How To Score Points
Raising Your Teen

*Understanding Your Teenager
in Today's Ever-Changing World*

Taylor DeBruce

i

ISBN-13: 978-1-7780600-0-7

Published by DLP publishing Canada

First Edition

Book Editor: Maryam Nawaz

Cover Design by Immaculate Studios

Dedication

I dedicate this book to the countless parents who, like me, have struggled with raising their teenage sons and daughters in different areas. Our journeys are different, but I have written this book, keeping you in mind.

Contents

v

Introduction

A few decades back (the 1980s to 1990s), you could prepare for teen years. You knew you had at least thirteen years before that teenage cloud hung over your home. After all, most kids started displaying typical teenage traits from twelve years from now on. If you were lucky enough, you'd only realize that your child no longer idolized you when they were fifteen. That's when you would start fretting over how many years you had until they turned eighteen and moved past that horrid stage.

But now? Kids are becoming teenagers much earlier (might it be something in the water?) Even your eight-year-old kid will scoff at you when you try to offer some advice.

Or blurt out that you're annoying them as they shun your kisses and hugs. It's getting much harder to hold on to these precious angels before that cloud hangs over your household.

It would be nice if we could tell that our lives were about to change in a millisecond. But how do you know you're under the dark cloud? Easy! You see it in the way your teenager acts. They are slamming doors, making a mess in their rooms, rolling their eyes, grunting at you, playing loud music, slouching, and acting out. Even when going out with friends, they call it 'hanging out' and will shoot daggers at you if you call it a play date. Does this describe your teenager? Have you caught yourself telling your child that they are now *acting like a teenager?* Have they suddenly changed? It's like you went to sleep one day and a stranger moved into your child's room, and you do not know *how* it all went wrong. All you know is that your child, who once longed for your hugs, now seems allergic to your affection. Even the teens who don't act out seem to shy away from their parents when the teenage bug hits them.

It's all normal, right? So, you figure you might as well get ahead of the curve and prepare for what's coming. The solution?–your friends who have an equally hard time raising their kids. That doesn't work. Even if they mean well, they are as confused as you are, trying to understand why their kids are running two Instagram accounts and only following them with one. You're there nodding, wondering how they ever got so lucky that their kids even follow them with one -yours won't even friend you on Facebook! So, you try the bookshop and go home with a couple of books that teach parents how to deal with teenagers. But none of these books address the problems facing Gen Zs. You turn one page after the other, shaken by how seemingly easier it was to raise a child in the twentieth century. *Do you mean these kids didn't even have cell phones? And oh, the parties were almost always a few streets away? My kid goes to parties across the state!*

The books are great, but they only push you closer to giving up. While teenage emotions and rage are similar, these books were for a very different generation. *The simpler times.* I know because I have been that frantic parent in the bookstore, reading the back covers and crossing my fingers that this would be the magic book. Sure, the books go into communication and how to deal with the raging emotions, but they barely scratch the surface.

Where's the book that tells you that some adult identifying as age-fluid will try to slide into your child's DMs? *How do you tell your kid that the other fifteen-year-old messaging them might be some thirty-six-year-old fronting as fifteen?* Or the one that tells you how to handle your fifteen-year-old being on contraceptives? What about the guide that takes you through what to do when your twelve-year-old discovers weed? Parenting in this twenty-first century is nothing like it was in the twentieth century. And expecting what worked a century ago to work now will only make your parenting journey harder. We're currently dealing with unlimited pornography access, coaxing our kids not to give in to the pressures of social media celebrities (don't get me started on the body distortion issues fueled by Instagram and TikTok influencers), and an age where children see the ills of society play out on live TV (how do you explain injustice-related protests to your fourteen-year-old who already has anxiety walking to the corner shop?) Unfortunately, these vices are not only affecting teenagers but adolescents and kids too. Our children are in danger!

You get the picture -we are dealing with a crisis. But what's the solution? If your teenager was back to being five and listened to everything you said, you could go back to childproofing the house. They were safer that way. But remember when you wanted your child to grow into a teen, eager to see what personality they would take on? That time has come! The good news is that most people grow out of their teenage personalities. They look back and go, 'what was I thinking?' The bad news is that this transition into adulthood can take a dark turn. But controlling your teenager is never the answer. Teenagers are reactionary -you push, they push harder. So, if you take that phone away, they will do what it takes to get online.

This book gets into what it's like to raise a Gen Z teenager and what it requires of you as a parent. Is there a way to guide your teenager without being that controlling parent that triggers childhood trauma? How can you protect your teenager while allowing them to stumble and make their mistakes? Is it too late to start parenting your teen? (Spoiler alert -you are never too late!)

It focuses on insights from experts as I lean on to my experiences as a parent. Does it mean you'll perfect the art of raising teens? Not even close, but you'll be a better parent where it counts. At the end of the day, parents are but custodians guiding children into adulthood. You might disagree with all your teenager's choices, but you'll be there supporting them each step of the way. The chapters in this book guide you on offering parental support without being overbearing or barely scratching the surface. I call it... The Balancing Act.

PS: All the chapters in the book cover integral teen parenting pain points, and you can read them in any order. Enjoy! I hope this book will inspire you as much as it inspired me as I wrote it.

Chapter One

Welcome To Parenting Gen Zs

Fewer than half (forty-seven percent) of Gen Zers say they're content with their lives compared to sixty percent of Millennials. And sixty-seven percent of Millennials believe that their life is full of purpose compared to only fifty-three percent of Gen Z.

What Makes Gen Zs Different?

Are you parenting a Gen Z teen? You've probably often wondered who is walking around your home -with headphones on, a distant look in their eyes, and a nonchalant approach to life. They seem to have a dramatically different view from yours. It does not matter if you're discussing politics, sexuality, careers, or hobbies. You always seem to be on different ends of the spectrum - it's almost like you're talking about life with an alien.

Tabloids and news outlets refer to this new generation as **millennials on steroids**. But what does that even mean? How do you even start to understand the fundamental differences between your teen and the average millennial? It begins with understanding what makes a generation. A generation is simply a group of people born within a similar period whose experiences shape how they view the world.

Here's an example—the millennials. This generation grew up during 9/11, bore the brunt of the great recession, and witnessed history in the making with the Obama election. Let's not forget that they grew up amidst the rise of the internet. Millennials are exceptional -I have raised one firsthand. I know how challenging it was to navigate the influence of the internet.

Then there are the Gen Xs. These grew up during the AIDS crisis, danced to MTV, and reveled at the end of the Cold War. Of course, their (our) parenting styles at the time borrowed a lot from the baby boomers who had grown up amidst assassinations, wars, protests, and presidential assassinations. Each generation has a tale that shapes its perspective. So, you can see where I am heading with this.

Gen Zs are the unique category we've got so far. They grew up in tandem with social media platforms. Add global terrorism, same-sex marriage rulings, and Trump's election to that list, and you've got them down to an art. But how has this shaped them?

While we cannot stereotype this generation and use a cookie-cutter parenting style on them, we can accept a few things:

- This generation has a weird fascination (obsession) with their smart devices. A good forty percent claim to be *addicted* to their devices!
- Gen Zs are highly entrepreneurial and want to jump into the job market as soon as possible. They are also pursuing more non-conventional careers—Instagram influencers, TikTok influencers, YouTube stars, and you name it!
- Their generation is highly competitive and more independent compared to millennials.

- Many Gen Zs struggle with mental health (most citing anxiety and depression). FOMO (fear of missing out) is more real in this generation than in any other era.

- Gen Zs are more open with their sexuality, shying away from labels and embracing gender fluidity and non-binary terms.

- Gen Zs view truth as relative. Rather than fall into the same religious patterns, we have seen in previous generations. They are more likely to do what does not hurt anyone than stick to what's carved in stone.

Why Previous Parenting Strategies Do Not Work?

Which generation do you think is the closest to Gen Zs? You'd be forgiven for citing millennials. After all, Gen Zs are *millennials on steroids*, but these two generations are worlds apart, as this book will reveal. Gen Zs are more in line with the Silent Generation. Oh yes, we're going back to the 1925 to 1945 generation, also known as *The Lucky Few Generation*. Here was a group of people who had just come from the First World War. As they picked up the pieces of their lives, they witnessed the Korean War, celebrated the moon landing, and sooner than they knew it, were smack in the middle of another World War.

But how can the Gen Zs relate to a generation that witnessed so much tragedy? The financial constraints. Both generations had to live in the ruins of a past they had no part in. For example, Gen Zs live in the effects of a past recession. No wonder they cannot help but do what they can to succeed in their careers. Oh, and Gen Zs get along well with baby boomers. So, you might notice that your teen gets along better with their grand or great-grandparents more than they do with you. Embrace it!

To parent your Gen Z, you would have to use strategies that worked back from 1925 to 1945. Even so, you must remember that the silent generation did not have the internet. They were not dealing with one crisis after the other playing out on a digital screen. They were sheltered to some effect, even with bullets raining down on villages and enemies dropping bombs. Why? They did not have pop-up notifications on everything wrong in the world. No news platform streamed breaking news throughout the day and night. Live streaming was unheard of. So, parents could decide just how much their children knew about the circumstances. They had the chance to break down each nugget into sizeable pieces of information for their young ones. But your teen does not have this protection. Parents are now watching their children's innocence stripped away from an early age. If you don't talk to them about something, someone else will, perhaps not as gently as you would like.

So, nothing that worked for the silent generation, millennials, or even baby boomers can prepare you for your Gen Z teen or tween. You need to arm yourself with a new set of parenting rules.

What Next for Gen Z Parenting?

As a parent (millennial or Gen X), you might be wondering how you can get through to a Gen Z teen if you can't use previous parenting strategies. Well, the Gen Z parenting map is quite complex. We are throwing helicopter parenting out and welcoming a more adaptive parenting technique. Why?

First, there's the fact that Gen Zs are highly independent and practical. They don't appreciate being told what to do and often do what feels right. Why? They have grown up in a society that tells them they have a voice, and they have learned how to use it. Some teens verbalize their rebellion, while others use artistic ways to express that they are not bending to your will. Whatever the case, the message will be clear. It's no longer a one-way street. So, folding your hands and having the last word does not cut it with them. For a parent, this can be incredibly scary. Most of us grew up in homes where our parents' word was the law. So, to parent a generation that can speak back is mind-boggling. Accepting that you are not lord over your teen is the first step towards hacking the Gen Z parenting puzzle. The next is to understand how to involve your teen in more decisions in the household.

Gen Zs have grown up in the era of social currency, with influencers paving the way for them. They have developed para-social relationships with these online personas who direct them on where to eat, shop, exercise, etc. Social media educates them on almost everything. So, you can't expect them to do precisely what you say. They've been clear that steamrolling won't work for them. What's the solution?–showing them! Practicing what you preach is the only way to go. I know it's a hard pill to swallow, but you can't be on TikTok all day and yelling at your tween to stay off their phone at the same time. Use the art of influence and mold them into *the adult* you want them to be.

I have emphasized that Gen Zs are independent, but that does not mean they know everything. They still need your guidance as they navigate the usual hurdles of being a teenager. They will face the same issues you did as a teen: peer pressure, body image issues, pressure to act like adults, sexual anxiety, and lack of confidence. The only difference is that their issues play out on a much bigger scale. Your teen's body image issues will only be made worse when they log on to social media and see a bunch of Instagram models showcasing their picture-perfect bodies. Accept that you cannot shield them from these influences and instead focus on helping them sort through their experiences.

Let's not forget that Gen Zs are at more risk of mental health issues. Most of them are going through or know someone struggling with anxiety and depression. Studies show a positive side to this—these teens have grown up in a society that allows them to express themselves. The result?–they will probably make much better parents than their predecessors. However, you need to understand how to help your teen through the mental health rollercoaster to get them there.

Are you ready? You might have thought that parenting a Gen Z teen would have been easier with all their independence and exposure. But it turns out that this is a double-edged sword. This book will show you how to make the best out of this turn of events.

***

Chapter Two

Parenting The Adolescent

"The bad thing about being my age is being expected to act like an adult at college/work but being treated like a child at home." —Seventeen-year-old

What is Adolescence?

When I think about adolescence, I think back to my science class when I was ten. Nobody had ever talked to me about my body—not my parents, relatives, or siblings. You'd think the church would have thrown some crumbs my way, but I had nothing. So, when my science teacher walked in with a stern smile on her face and a book in hand, I was not prepared for what was coming.

She pointed out the changes that would occur in our bodies, and I could feel my classmates somewhat changing their postures. They sat with their backs hunched and their chins so low that it was impossible not to assess what they were feeling—shame. We had grown up in a society where these changes were not discussed at the dinner table. So, to have a teacher walk in and look you in the eye, telling you that your body was about to change, was a game-changer.

In those days, if you were lucky, your parents would throw a few pointers at you at the oddest of moments. You'd be fixing a light bulb in the garage, and your dad would go, "Eh, stay away from boys. You're a big girl now." Before you even thought of an answer, he'd be gone. A few weeks would go by, and as the horror of the last conversation washed off your face, your mom would go, "Here, I got something for you." Then you'd open the package and find a pack of tampons. I was red-faced for most of my teenage years because sexuality was taboo. So, you picked up bits of information here and there and read science books like they had the key to a magic portal. Because they did, they unlocked the mystery that was adolescence.

What followed were hushed conversations between peers. Have your pubic hairs grown in? When do you think you will get your period? Did you hear Mark's voice in class? I think his voice broke! A few giggles here and there, and we thought we'd uncovered a state secret. Little did we know that adolescence went beyond the physical, and that's the part our science teacher left out, a part that haunted us for many years.

Can we make the same mistakes with Gen Zs? No! As I said earlier, they have access to this information. They may even know more than you do (it probably scares you to hear that, but that's the world we live in now).

The Transition: Preparing for the Roller Coaster Ahead

"Adolescence lasts longer these days, as people go to university and do internships, and need more support from parents." —Teen

The best way to describe adolescence is a transitional period between childhood and adulthood. Let's assume your child travels through a portal. So, one minute your kid is eight, and you're shuffling them into the portal, and the next, they are twenty and coming out as an adult. In between those years, they undergo changes that shape the person they become.

Oh, and here's the best part of it—you never know when your kid falls into that portal. Some fall into it at twelve, others head in at nine, and the slower ones moonwalk their way to it at thirteen or even later. But you will hardly know when it happens. You wake up one day and go, '*who are you?*' to the moody bearded teenager walking through your hallway. They, of course, are just as confused as you are. If you're not careful, the transitional period can be akin to two ships passing in the night—one with a distressed captain looking for a map and fumbling with the signals and controls and the other captain lost in memories, wishing they could turn back the time and go back to the simpler times.

But your baby, with the wide smile and eager hugs, is not coming back. You are now dealing with an adolescent who will rebel every chance they get as they try to figure out who they want to be. If you're lost in the past's glory, you will miss out on the present, and that will affect both you and your child's future. So, focus on the iron that's melting right in front of you, and enjoy the smelting process, shaping that iron into the perfect mold (adult).

How To Prepare Your Child for Adolescence

"We spend most of our lives as adults, so it's important to understand what happens before, and how it impacts adulthood." —**Girl, Seventeen-year-old**

Most of the people I talked to when writing this book agreed with me on one thing—we need to do better when parenting our adolescents. We cannot hide behind the notion that science teachers and school counselors will carry the bigger bulk of the work. Our kids are learning about their bodies from as early as four! So, before your kid's science teacher is flipping through the pages and delving into the physical and psychological changes, your kid will know it all. You can only hope that they will know the right thing and not be led by the misinformation out there. Just because our kids have access to information does not mean it's the *correct* information. Here's what I think of the information reaching our kids:

Suddenly, the Lie jumps out of the well, puts on the clothes of the Truth, and runs off towards a nearby village. The furious Truth leaps out of the well and runs to find the Lie and get her clothes back. Seeing the Naked Truth, the

Villagers are horrified and look away with contempt and rage. The poor Truth returned to the well and disappeared, forever hiding her shame. And since that day, the lie travels the world, clothed as the Truth.

It's an excerpt from *The Naked Truth and the Lie*, a story as old as time and one that continues to inspire the need to question our sources of information. You get the gist—lies spread faster than the truth, so what your child may think they know about their bodies could be a bunch of hogwash. So, how do you replace lies with the truth?

Nine To Eleven Years

Whoa! Are we *really* talking to our kids about their bodies as young as nine? Oh, yes!–If recent studies are anything to go by, we might even start as young as seven in the coming years. Kids are developing fast, and their bodies show signs of puberty as young as nine. Can we put this on climate change? Who knows? But as we figure out where to point our fingers, let's see what you can expect of your kids:

- Their friendships will be more solid by now, and you'll notice a pattern in these relationships. They will hang around the same group of kids from whom they derive their social status.

- Peer pressure also sneaks in at this point. Don't be surprised if they dress and speak differently.

- Unfortunately (and this is big), now is when they realize their bodies are different. So, it would help if you watched out for any signs of eating disorders and body dysmorphia (I will get into this later).

- They are more independent and prefer to handle some things on their own.

- The best part is your kid can *actually* listen to you for much longer–yay for an increased attention span! It won't last long, so make the most of it.

What Role Do You Play in This?

You're at the easy stage. It's all about being involved at this point. You can:

- **Spend more time with your child**. Encourage them to make more friends to broaden their social interactions. Limit their screen time to enable them to be more present. Be careful to avoid the notion of punishment rather than discipline. One promotes open communication, and the other shuts that door.

- **Cheer them on as they take on more extracurricular activities.** A healthy body and mind will equal a more balanced child. Add a healthy diet and enough sleep (9-12 hours), and your kid will be okay.

- **Be open about the dangers of social pressures.** Talk about sex, drugs, eating disorders, social media, etc. Please get to know what they think and take them through the effects of engaging in such activities.

- **Embrace their independence.** Carve out more roles for them in the home. Also, teach them how to set and stick to goals, even if it's as simple as making their bed each morning.

- **Bring in the aspect of affirmations.** Most of us grew up with our parents doting on us. Then, when they were no longer around to praise us, we crumbled, unsure whether we were still good girls and boys. Teach children to praise themselves when they have done an excellent job. This self-affirmation will still be around even when you are not.

- **Open up about finances.** Gen Zs are more entrepreneurial than the previous generations. They leave high school and hit the ground running with their careers. So, this might be the right time to prepare your kid finance-wise. Bring out your savings and expenses calculator and teach your child how to budget.

- **Bring out the rules.** Now that they can understand right and wrong, you can bring out the rules. Again, keep in mind that this is a Gen Z, so you need to spell out the reasons for the rules. For example, if no parent is in the home, you cannot hold a party. Then get into the why. You need to be creative and compelling with your whys.

- **Get into what they could experience in puberty.** What emotional changes might they notice? Are there any physical changes heading their way? What can they do to navigate each of these changes? You might need to use a diagram for pictorial references -make it a bit like a science class. I need to add that you might want to take it slowly instead of bombarding your kid with all the information. But if they can take it, why not?

Twelve To Fourteen Years

Okay, now we're at the stage where most parents are forced to deal with the fact that they have a teenager in the house. It's impossible to deny the obvious -the facial hair, the breasts, the monthly tampon expenses, the deep voice, you know how it goes. Your teenager can also see what's happening, and they know that everyone else can, too. So, you can imagine just how conscious they are of their appearance. You were too once, so you know how exposed your child may be feeling. You need to act fast to ensure that they don't use drugs or fall into other bad habits to escape their reality. So, how do you know that your kid is smack in the middle of puberty?

- **Your teen cares about how they look.** They spend hours agonizing about their clothes and general body image. Does this make me look fat? Is this even trendy? If you make me wear that to school tomorrow, I will kill myself!

- **Their moods are like a pendulum, akin to being stuck on a banana ride.** One minute, they are professing their love for you, and the next, they are slamming the door in your face! Oh, and they have short tempers, like faulty fuses -one wrong word, and you have it coming.

- **Your opinion matters less than that of your children's friends.** They no longer come to you for advice. You're the moneybags, and their friends are the advisors -roles have changed. And when you try to step in and offer an idea about their style, hair, or even makeup, you get an eye roll, shrug, just something to show you that you are punching above your weight class.

- **Schoolwork stresses them, and they can't seem to keep up with the workload.** Your child constantly worries about assignments and needs more help to get things done.

- **Their independence is at a higher level.** They show more confidence in setting goals and sticking to them. They also start expressing their future expectations with these big plans, like becoming an actor, singing on Broadway, moving to Manhattan, etc.

- **Their eating habits may have changed.** Your child could eat everything in sight or could fiddle with their food at dinner. The other day, a friend told me that her twelve-year-old niece wouldn't eat because she does not want to be fat! So, there's a sign of an eating disorder at such an early age.

- **Your teen may feel sad or depressed and may seem to move through life lost.** Unfortunately, it's a gateway to drugs, unsafe sex, truancy, and a hoard of other problems. Now might be the time to pay more attention to their moods and expressions. You could notice something that has not caught your eye in the past.

Should You Wait It Out?

How amazing would it be if you could step back these few years and watch the puzzle come together? But you can't. Now, more than ever, you need to be present in your child's life as it affects their future. Any habits they sink into now could tug at them well into adulthood. You can always turn the outcome around by:

- **Getting to know your child's friends.** It's always nice to get a feeling about the people whose company your child enjoys. It gives you a glimpse of what matters to your child and enables you to influence your kid by influencing their social group. Advise your child to stick to friends who influence positive changes in their life.

- **Being open about drugs, sex, eating disorders, social media, etc.** Teens at this stage can understand what all these categories entail. They also know enough about these activities and can give you a breakdown of their take on these matters. Listen to them and be honest about how you feel about these sensitive topics. You should not shy away because that avoidance could push them further away from you.

- **Taking part in their school life.** You are not yet off the hook for those parent-teacher conferences or parent-child workshops. Find out what more you can do at school and hang around more often. Sure, your kid might roll their eyes at you chaperoning an activity, but it gives you more time together. Don't be the snooping parent who's there to police everything they do.

- **Allowing them to take over the reins in their life.** Your child is now more confident in their decisions. Your role is to guide them in making the best ones while respecting their opinions. Learn to communicate with your child. For example, if your kid wants to use all their savings to buy a car, talk to them about why you think it's a bad idea or otherwise. Don't tell a Gen Z what to do -consider their thoughts and feelings and have an open dialogue. Else, they will buy the car and stash it in some park–these kids!

- **Enforcing boundaries.** You need to step up as a parent and mark out what's acceptable in the household. That includes household duties, school achievements, dialogues with other household members, screen time, etc. You are still the parent, even with your teen taking on more responsibility. That's a role you should not delegate or neglect.

- **Walking them through the effects of their physical changes.** Is your teen too shy to leave the house when they have a zit? Are they hiding at home because they are afraid of people's reactions to their physical changes? Your teen will need a lot of reassurance, and you'll need to step in quite a lot. Talk to them about even the most embarrassing of changes and if you don't know the answer, find it together.

- **Tracking your teen.** You can't afford not to know where your teen is. Teenagers need structure. You should know where they will be, how you can reach them, what time they will get home, if they made it to school, etc. You should also set rules for what they should do when home alone. How do they handle emergencies? Can they have friends over?

- **Encouraging physical activity.** How do you deal with that pent-up energy coursing through your teen's veins? You direct it to a sport. It could be anything from walking the dog to playing football on the weekends. Couple this with limited screen time, healthy meals, and enough sleep (8-10 hours).

Fifteen To Seventeen Years

Do you want proof that girls mature faster than boys? Here's a fact -most girls will have completed puberty by the time they are fifteen. They will already master their menstrual cycle, choosing to fit bras, and dealing with their fleeting crushes. But your son? He'll just have entered the actual depths of puberty. Does that mean that your daughter will be in the clear? Not even close. Now is when she'll start noticing cellulite on her thighs and taping her legs together to create the illusion of perfection—or skipping a meal to avoid bloating. Maybe she'll get on her first diet -it could even be the cabbage soup diet! And your son? He'll probably be lifting weights, trying out protein shakes, or eating more than he did before. Or he could agonize about why his skin is not as smooth anymore or why he can't pull off a ponytail. Welcome to the last teen years, the most challenging part of navigating teen years.

What Are You In For?

Your teen will:

- **Start exploring their sexuality and romantic relationships at this point.** Gone are the days when you were sure your daughter would introduce you to some lanky boy from the block. Now, it could be anyone, including her best friend Angie from first grade. Or she could realize that she does not feel comfortable being labeled as a woman. You'll also be part of this exploration, so it's time you keep an open mind.

- **Be less confrontational.** You notice your teen will be more open to engaging with you, allowing you to impact their lives positively. But it would help if you met them where they are rather than tell them.

- **Still be showing signs of independence** and will want to carve out a path by themselves.

- **Probably experience feelings of sadness and could sink into depression.** You'll need to be the guiding force that helps them out of this funk. The alternative will be drug abuse, truancy, unsafe sex, etc.

How Do You Step into All of This?

Seeing your child changing right in front of your eyes can be daunting. Here's how you can make this process easier for all of you:

- **Keep paying attention to their social and academic interests.** Whether they are getting into theater or pursuing art, be the person who pushes them to stick to their interests.

- **Praise your teen even as you encourage self-affirmation.** They still need to hear that echo blazing behind them, assuring them they are loved and accepted.

- **Pay attention to their behaviors.** Are they eating less? Do they have friends? Are they going on about how life has no meaning? Figure out if your teen is struggling and if you can't offer them the help they need, seek a counselor to step in.

- **Understand that your teen is more independent now and has opinions about life.** Learn to listen to them, even though you may disagree on the best path for them. Also, encourage your child to develop problem-solving and conflict resolution skills.

- **Gauge their internet use.** How are they using social media? Are they spending too much time on these platforms? Guide them on making the best decisions when interacting with people on the internet -what to post, when to involve an adult, when to walk away, etc.

- **Don't forget to talk about sensitive topics like drugs, sex, and eating disorders.** Ideally, you will have spoken to your child about these from ages nine, but even if you are starting now, you still have a lot of good you can impart in their life.

- **Treat your teen like one they have a right to privacy.** Respect their space. Don't barge into their room without knocking, read their diary, or snoop into their direct messages.

- **Encourage a healthy lifestyle** more nutritious meals, enough sleep, more exercise, etc.

You might have noticed that the emphasis on physical changes has taken a bit of a backseat with Gen Z parenting. So, why is it on the back burner? For a simple reason - physical changes are but a fraction of what kids go through in adolescence. Mostly, they struggle with peer pressure, the need to act like adults, eating disorders, sexual health, academic achievements, concerns about their future, social media influences, etc. It's even worse for Gen Zs who now deal with social currency -where they ate, who they were with, where they hung out, etc. *If you didn't post it, then it didn't happen.* So, the acne on their face or their voices breaking in recess is just part of the whole enigma that is adolescence. And as a parent, you can't pick one struggle and stick with it. You must embrace the entire experience and feel its depth and weight. That's the only way you can truly be there for your teenager.

Are You Making Your Child's Changes About You?

"Adolescence isn't a negative word; it's the surrounding words that are negative, like immaturity and lack of independence."

There's a reason so many authors have penned down guides to parenting teens. It's a lot of trial and error, and nobody is sure they're doing the right thing. You second-guess yourself, questioning if you've done enough for your child while pulling your hair out at their antics. How can you ensure that you're not the parent throwing a tantrum at their kid each time things go wry?

- **Calm Down:** Sometimes, you feel the need to push back. Rather than follow your kid into the gutters to have the final word, stop and breathe.
- **Listen:** I know it feels great to be correct. But what's the point if being right only pushes your child further away from you? Learn to welcome your child's insights

even when you are sure you're right. The whole point lies in reaching a consensus as often as you can.

- **Love Your Child:** Parenting is not a conditional contract. You can't only love your child when they do what you say, then reject them when they rebel. Talk to your child. Instead of labeling them a bad child, try something like, "I don't know why you thought sneaking out in the dead of night to see your friends was a good idea. But I am sure you have a reasonable point of view. All I want is for you to take better care of yourself."

- **Loosen the Reins:** You've been the law for a long time, and it's hard to accept that your child now wants independence. Rather than refuse them this right, set boundaries. Come up with a plan that works for both of you. For example, maybe your child can leave home as long as they are contactable for their away hours.

- **Aim to Understand:** It's not easy to be rational when you find your fourteen-year-old passed out on the kitchen floor, drunk as a skunk. But ask yourself, what are they trying to achieve? They are probably looking for attention, social currency, and a break from school.

What is it? Talk to them and figure it out. It might surprise you that your child is crying for help.

Monkey See, Monkey Do!

Oh, and seeing as you're raising a Gen Z, none of the above measures will work if you're not an exemplary role model. Don't snack on chips and soda all weekend, and advise your kid to grab some broccoli. It won't work. This generation will let no one steamroll them, including their parents. So, if you want them to do something, show them what that looks like. I know how times have changed!

So, you're probably wondering how you can talk to your kid about sex and mental health. I have covered this in the later chapters of this book, giving you a detailed guide on broaching these sensitive topics. But first, let's get to a core subject: are you treating your teens the same?

***

Chapter Three

Are Boys And Girls All That Different?

*"I'm a man, and I enjoy watching ballet and listening to Taylor Swift. Art appreciation is not gender-specific." –***Arjun Jagdish Ram**

The #*GenderBender* campaign is one of the many movements that have caught my eye in recent years. People are moving away from gender stereotypes, and I am here for it. Young girls don't have to dress up as princesses for Halloween, nor do young boys need to be spidermen. Our children are now choosing who they want to be. I take back to my son's early years when we lived in a gayborhood in Vancouver. Most of the cute spots in the area were dotted with men and women openly expressing their love for each other. So, as we sat in one of these restaurants enjoying a quiet afternoon, my son looked up at me in amazement. He was pointing at a couple behind me, eyes wide open, and asking, "Why are those two men kissing each other?" I casually glanced at the couple in question, two young men embroiled in a passionate kiss, then to my son, and answered, "Because it's okay for two men to kiss each other."

That was back in the early 2000s when LGBTQIA+ rights were barely a thing. Most people did not understand why a man would choose to be with another man or why a woman would love her fellow woman. But I knew it was my duty as a parent to pass on the right message to my son— acceptance and love for everyone. Even now, as he's matured into a fine young man, I can see that my lesson back then bore the fruit I wanted. I could have been the intolerant human who fed my child with poisonous perceptions. However, I fought the stereotype for my child's good.

What choices are you making as a parent? What messages are you passing on to your child about gender identity, sexuality, and gender roles?

What is Gender Identity?

"If two girlfriends kiss each other, they're oh-so-cute and besties, and the world is XOXOXO about that concept, but if two guy friends kiss each other, they're gay and uncool. There's nothing wrong with a little of bromance." **–Rushil Zutshi, Vellore Institute of Technology**

Remember when speeches all started with 'ladies and gentlemen?' Well, that does not work anymore. You can't assume that someone identifies as male and creates an email with dear sir. Or tap the lady in line and go, "excuse me, miss." Such assumptions can land you in trouble in the workplace or social settings. So, if you can't make this faux pas elsewhere, why would you do it in your home? Have you explored your child's gender identity?

I know I might have lost you here, so I will take it slow. Gender and sex are not the same. Sex is the label you get at birth -male or female, based on your sexual organs. But gender refers to your social status -how society expects you to behave because of your sex. Can you see the relation? If I were to be the traditional parent, I would have pushed my son to play sports because that's what other boys were expected to do. Gender also encompasses legal status -you are a boy or a girl, man, or woman. That means that if you are a woman, you will fulfill women's roles in society. It's that simple -or at least that's what society forced down our throats in the past centuries.

It wasn't until a few decades ago that people started differentiating sex, gender, and gender identity. Gender identity is all about how you feel inside. Some people feel like they are male, while others identify as female. If your gender identity aligns with your assigned sex, you fall under the cisgender category. Others feel like masculine females or feminine males. And that's where we land on transgender people, who feel that their assigned sex differs from who they are. Finally, some people don't identify as any of the sexes. That's where gender fluidity comes in–that's why you cannot assume that someone answers to miss or mister.

Let's use a typical example. Your child's sex can be male, and society expects them to run around chasing lizards and playing tag. But inside, your child feels like a Barbie doll and wants to act and dress like one. So, they use your makeup, asking for Barbie-like clothes and acting like a real-life Barbie doll. It's one example, but you get the gist.

So, how long do you have before you talk with your kid? Newsflash -gender identity begins as early as two years! Your tween or teen is probably aware of pronouns and gender identity. But are they questioning their identity? Do they feel like something is different about them? There's only one way to find out:

- **Understand gender identity:** You cannot educate or resonate with your kid if you don't understand gender identity and sexual orientation differences. Unfortunately, people often get it mixed up. For example, you might assume he wants to date a male because your son identifies as female. But gender identity does not make sexuality.

- **Learn the terms:** From sex to gender fluidity to gender nonbinary down to assigned sex, learn what each term entails. The more you know, the more valuable your conversation will be.

- **Brush up on sexual identity:** Do you know what it means to be pansexual? How about bisexual? Most people get lost in the LGBTQIA+ terms because they cannot tell each one apart. Learn these too.

- **Create a conducive environment:** You can't walk up to your daughter and go, "Hey, do you know what a lesbian is?" Catching them off-guard will not work as the conversation could go left. So instead, ease them into it. For example, you could watch a movie together and say something like, "I love how TV shows are now embracing different sexual identities." Then if your child shows interest in the conversation, you can take it from there.

- **Encourage openness:** When your child finally opens up to talking to you, let them know your door is always open.

- **Accept help:** If your child is uncomfortable talking to you, they might confide in a relative or teacher. Let the confidant know you would be open to discussing it with your child when you find out. You can also enlist the help of a therapist if your child is not comfortable broaching this matter with you.

- **Be cautious:** Teens can be susceptible to how you refer to them. So, if your kid comes out and says that they will use the pronoun 'they,' please stick to it. Don't refer to them as 'she' or 'he' when they have stipulated what they prefer.

In all this, be the supportive parent who showers their kid with love and support. It will be a terrifying experience for them, so try not to make it about you. If you are having a hard time, seek help to avoid projecting your concerns on your child.

Gender Roles: Do They Still Exist?

"I love wearing pink kurtas and Pink shirts. Not because I'm Gay. Not Because I'm feminine, but because I like it. Pink is a color, not an identity." – **Vignesh Hariharan, MSR Law**

I grew up being told to act or dress a certain way because of my gender. So, I vowed not to subject my child to the same. Why? Gender stereotypes are harmful because they bar people from being who they want to be. Men are expected to be aggressive and oversee the finances, home repairs, and everything that requires strength. Their appearances should also follow a specific manual like short hairstyles, pants in tow, covering a thick muscular build. Women?–they should sit pretty and patient, nurturing their children and bearing the emotional strain and accommodating, taking on the more 'feminine' careers like nursing and teaching while maintaining an hourglass body.

So, what happens if you don't fit into these stereotypes? Society chastises you for it. You can't be a man and bawl even when things go wrong. Or be a woman who is intelligent and assertive. No! You must fit into a box, and if you don't, society will beat you into it. Do you want to know the worst part? Gender stereotypes start at home. It begins with you asking your daughter to clean the house while your son sits playing video games. Or enforcing different curfews for your kids -your son can stay out until midnight, but your daughter must be home by nine.

We no longer live in a world where gender stereotypes contribute anything meaningful to our lives. Look around you. How many men are now opting to stay home and be stay-at-home dads? Have you noticed the number of women chasing the bag instead of starting a family at a young age? What about career choices? Men and women are running for the same positions. I don't want to paint the picture of gender equality in the workplace as we are not yet there, but we are headed there. So, you cannot bury your head in the sand and propagate gender stereotypes in your home. Hyper-masculinity and hyper-femininity are slowly being phased out. And here's how you can play a part in this movement:

- **Be a role model to your kids:** You must lead by example as a Gen Z parent. You can't berate someone for their gender identity, then come home and ask your kids to shun gender stereotypes. It starts with treating everyone equally. Also, watch how you speak. For example, you can't say things like, "I am a woman. I can't change the light bulb on my own", then expect your daughter to think that home repairs are not gender-specific.

- **Show fairness:** Do you need to share out the duties? How about you send your son to make dinner and have your daughter mow the lawn? Have your kids done something wrong? Ensure that their discipline relates to their actions and not their genders. Fathers often go easy on the girls, and moms are known to baby their sons. Please don't do it.

- **Call out stereotypes:** Whether it's in a movie or a picnic with friends or even at home, call out stereotypical people. You might even need to call yourself out now and then. Don't sit back as people make sexist jokes and think your silence speaks volumes. It does not.

Here's some homework: Try something different at home. Say, for example, that you have not changed your child's diaper and always delegate this to your partner. Take on this role and show your partner and other children that you do not subscribe to gender roles.

Write five things you don't do at home or work because they do not align with your gender identity. Have your children do the same thing. Then do these things and hold yourself and your kids accountable.

The Danger of Double Standards

"In a society that pressurizes men to be in control of a wedding proposal and follow a two-month salary rule for the ring, I'm a woman, and I proposed to my husband and bought my wedding ring." —Esha Agarwal Gejji

Have you ever noticed how some parents treat their kids differently? Some don't even know that they are doing it. They have somehow been conditioned by society that it's the right way to do things. So, they keep doing it, unaware that they are damaging their children. What am I talking about?

Setting Their Sons on Pedestals

Sons have always been heirs. Ergo, bearing a son has always been a bigger blessing than a daughter. A man could have ten daughters with his wife, but he would try just one more time to get that coveted heir -leave alone if this decision put his wife's health at risk. He would do everything it took, including remarrying ten times over, just to have someone who would carry his legacy. And when he finally bore this son, the daughters would fade into oblivion as the son took his rightful place -showered with gifts and bathed in affection.

Has the modern world changed this? No, parents still crave a son. They somehow believe that sons are more gifted than daughters. Ask a parent what they expect their son to be–an engineer, a pilot, a world leader. And the daughter?–a model, a stewardess, a rich man's wife, perhaps. Unbeknownst to these parents, they set the bar low for their daughters, inevitably setting them up for failure.

Different Forms of Appreciation

I read an interesting story the other day. A young mother was angry at how people treated her daughter differently based on her clothes. People would applaud the kid for almost anything when she was in unisex clothes, assuming that she was male. They'd say things like *he's such an intelligent little boy. He would make an outstanding athlete. Look at him catch the ball with such speed!* But when she dressed her daughter as a girl, people would coo at the child as *she's so pretty. Look at how beautiful she looks in that dress. Oh, how graceful she is!*

Are you guilty of the same? Be honest. Studies show that process praise (how you praise a child for their efforts) differs between boys and girls. Boys are encouraged to do better, boosting their confidence. But girls are brought up knowing that their strength lies in their grace and beauty and that intelligence has little to do with it. So, the boys take up math, and the girls pursue arts -a tale as old as time.

Educational Expectations Differ

How many parents encourage their daughters to take up advanced courses? Look at the STEM spaces. So many qualified women have been locked out of these spaces -not because they were not good enough to make it, but because they were conditioned to believe they didn't have what it took. Most parents quickly assume that their sons are intelligent and that their daughters need more time to process things. They believe that intelligence is inherent in boys and that girls should pursue easier courses. What does that do to your children? It frustrates the boys who must live up to these unbelievable expectations and limits how far girls can go.

Again, are you guilty of these parenting oversights?

Varying Investments into Kids

Here's another interesting finding: parents are more likely to show up for school activities when they have a son. Again, that inherent belief that their sons show promise propels them to be there for them. But with daughters, parents are more likely to assume that the child will grow out of the phase. *So, she enjoys playing the clarinet. Eh, I guess we'll see how long it lasts.*

Parents, especially fathers, have also been found guilty of investing more time in their sons. They somehow believe that they need more attention to nurture their raw talents. So, they keep showing up for them. Unfortunately, their daughters must make do with the little attention they get. And sometimes, they act up, hoping to get more time with their parents.

You might not intend to treat your kids differently, but you could have. Each time you put one gender on a pedestal, you diminish the other, affecting their social and economic development. But you're not only affecting the overlooked gender; you are also putting too much pressure on the one on the pedestal.

Can you come up with instances where you have treated your son and daughter differently?

When to Treat Boys and Girls Differently

"People keep telling me I need to learn how to cook only because I'm a woman. I don't like cooking, and I don't want to learn how to make round rotis (chapati), just Maggi. A woman's place is not just in the kitchen." –Poorna Mujumdar

If you look up parenting boys versus girls, you'll start seeing the patterns of gender stereotypes. For example, some people believe boys are harder to parent, while others think girls are harder. But these are some stereotypes we embrace from an early age. So, parents start coming down hard on the gender they believe is more problematic. But have you ever considered that our parenting styles might be to blame for these differences?

Here's an example. Jane grows up in a home where she's taught to be feminine. You know how it goes -be quiet, do what you're told and watch your waistline. It works for a long time. Then she gets to her teen years with acne and weight gain in tow. She no longer feels like the picture of femininity and is now struggling with a hoard of mental issues. So, what's keeping her from doing what it takes to fit the picture? Maybe a skipped meal here and there. Or she could rebel against these stereotypes and try to prove her independence so much that she harms herself.

Is there a way we can avoid damaging our kids? Should we parent them using the same manual? Should Jane and her brothers be subject to the same parenting books?

Now, this might be a bit confusing. On the one hand, treat your children equally by affording them the same academic and career opportunities, showering them with equal levels of affection, and being present for all of them. But they are still different. Your daughter will not face the same challenges as your son because society will treat them differently. So, when should you treat them differently? Here's the answer. When undoing the harm that society has rained down on them or undoing the harm that you, as the parent, may have caused in their earlier years.

What Parenting Styles Can You Embrace for Girls?

"I'm a woman, and I follow the latest books, not the latest fashion trends." **–Sharada Srinivasan, National Law School**

What messages do you need to communicate to your daughter that you will not face with your son?

- **Femininity is a choice:** Your daughter does not have to spend her life being passive and walking on eggshells that she can be loud and proud and walk into a room with her head high and chest out.
- **She can be anything she wants to be:** She can stay home and raise her kids or can be a CEO, or can spend her time traveling the world.
- **She's smart enough**: She can take on STEM careers, lead the world, or start a business from scratch.
- **Her sexuality is hers:** She can choose what she can do with her body as long as she is safe.

- **Her consents matter:** That nobody may hit her or have their way with her without her consent.

- **Her body belongs to her:** Nobody may tell her what to do with it.

- **Sports are not just for boys:** She can join a team or play an individual sport if she wants to.

- **Speak for yourself:** She can always say 'no' and walk away.

Should You Parent Your Sons Differently from Your Daughters?

"It is tragic how certain facial expressions are only imputed to a particular gender. We are men, and we are more than happy to pout for the camera and break another gender stereotype. And we do it in pink!" –Shobhit Singh Ranawat, Girish Ashok, RVCE

We have grown up in a society that conditions men to be pillars of strength, to the detriment of their mental health. So, what should you tell your boys?

- That they can like cute animals, dress in pink if that's what makes them happy, and that it's okay if they want to play with dolls and sleep with teddy bears in their bed.

- Expressing emotions is not a sign of weakness, and crying is okay.
- They don't have to chase the 9-5 and choose to stay home and raise babies instead.
- Seeking mental health help is a brave move, and society should not tell them otherwise.
- It's not okay to hit anyone even if they disagree: they must honor people's boundaries.
- Girls are people and should be treated with respect and not objectified.
- Consent is necessary each time they want to be intimate with their partners, both on their side and their partner's.

These are the conversations you must have with your kids –conversations most of us never had with our parents. When your child feels safe to break the gender stereotypes, you get to enjoy their individuality. However, you set them free from the shackles of these stereotypes, enabling them to be who they truly are.

Have you had these conversations with your teens?

***

Chapter Four

What Is Your Teenager Thinking? Unlocking The Teenage Brain

There are known knowns, known unknowns, and unknown unknowns.

I watched a past season of Boondocks when one character said this statement which had me thinking.

There are things we can all accept that we know the sun rises from the east, then those we know we don't know, like how many more planets there are in this universe. Then, (the big one) the things we don't even know about! It honestly blew my mind.

Then I reflected on my life and could see just how true this statement was. Why? Every few years, Google Photos reminds me of a photo that I took on a day like this X number of years ago. It goes, "Hey, look at this picture of you three years ago" or "here you were seven years ago." I follow the prompt and stare at this picture of me smiling, and in each, I can swear that I think I know all there is to life. And each time, I am amazed at how little I knew about what life was back then. It's pretty amazing, isn't it? To be so oblivious to the reality that we don't know.

Even now, I'm sure I don't know even half of it. But that's how life works. We think that when we've faced adversity and come out on the other end, we've somehow hacked life.

This thinking probably reared its head when I was a teen and thought I'd finally discovered the secret to life–that adults knew nothing about what they were talking about. I've seen it in many kids. They go about life convinced that they know something we don't. But unfortunately, others can't keep up with the life-changing experiences coming their way, so they opt-out, somehow losing themselves in it all.

Where is your teen in all this? What can you do to help them through it?

Teenage Perspectives on Life

Known Knowns: things we know we know.

You've put in the work and outlined the best decisions your child can make. Maybe you've even gone as far as stating the pros and cons of what you're advising them to do. *Eating veggies will strengthen your immune system to perform better at sports. Less screen time allows you to sleep better.* Then you come home and find your child doing the opposite. A few deep breaths later, you are back at it, advising them and hoping that you will make some headway this time. You're frustrated and cannot help but agonize on why they can't seem to toe the line. *Are they just testing you? Why can't they see that you're only trying to do what's best for them?* Perturbed and even heartbroken, you reach out to other parents. They are also having a rough time with their teens, maybe even worse than you have it. So, you can't help but think that it's a teenage phase that will pass—and you're right!

I've been through the wringer too and had to ask myself some hard questions about why my teen would not listen to me. Countless books, podcasts, GP sessions, and even soul-searching retreats later, and I pinned down why teens think they know everything in life. It turns out that their prefrontal cortex is still undeveloped at this stage. Not that there is something wrong with them, it's just another development phase in the transition from childhood to adulthood. But without a developed prefrontal cortex, they have little to keep them from giving in to their impulses. It's why your child may have an exam tomorrow and still thinks it's a good idea to go partying all night.

It's not that teens don't hear what you're saying; they *just* don't have the brainpower (if we can call it that) to do the right thing all the time. So, your teen will face issues with:

- **Planning:** You see how you can plan your week. Teens may face issues with this. It's not unheard of for them to schedule conflicting tasks, e.g., dinner with you, a date with a friend, and a tutor session. It can happen a lot and can even be annoying. But remember that sometimes, they have no control over their impulses - they could just be saying yes to everything!

- **Processing Emotions:** As an adult, you learn to keep your cool. You know that not every action warrants a reaction, which helps you avoid most nasty encounters. But your teen? Managing emotions is a foreign concept. So, they yell back, act out, slam doors, walk out, scream, cry, bang on tables, threaten to run away -you know the drill. And sometimes, it's just because you asked them if they had a good day in school. You never know what to expect.

- **Selflessness:** Your teen is a long way from learning how to walk in other people's shoes. It's not a lie that most teens are preoccupied with their lives -their clothes, friends, and school. It's always about them. So, when you need something from them, they look at it as a punishment rather than a way to help out in the house. For example, you could ask your child to mow the lawn, only to be met with an *"I am always doing things in this house. Why do you hate me?"*

- **Morality and Consequences:** Most people feel a tinge of guilt when they lie, even to get out of tricky situations. But teens rarely do. They will do or say what it takes to get what they want. That's why it's so easy for them to make fake IDs and show up in clubs, knowing fully well that they should not be there. Their conscience has still not set in because they don't understand the gravity of their actions.

So, while you may think that your kid is acting out, it's because they haven't grasped what life entails. They are still developing. And here's the best part. This process continues until they are twenty-five. That's why so many young adults start turning their lives around in their mid-twenties -they can finally think clearly.

What do you do in the meantime as you wait for nature to work its magic? You guide your teen, correcting the behavior and not taking it out on your child. Even when you feel like pulling your hair out and having a tantrum, remember that you're the one with the developed prefrontal cortex.

The Fear of the Unknown

Known Unknowns: *Things that we Know we Don't Know*

When your teen is not busy listening to Billie Eilish or dancing on TikTok, what's going through their mind? Most parents think their kids romanticize their crushes and plan their outfits. So, they believe that if they cover those pain points, their kids will be okay. But that's not the case. After 9/11, children were now facing fears that other generations had not encountered. While other generations had survived wars, the youths' pressures had now changed. In a survey held in 2005, most teens stated they were afraid of terror attacks. The next top concerns were spiders, death, failing in life, war, heights, gang violence, being alone, and the real world. It's interesting that sometimes as parents, we forget our kids could be as worried as we are about their future.

Have things changed in 2021? Are our kids less terrified than they were almost two decades ago? Sadly not. Our children are losing sleep over:

- **Climate Change:** Did you know that most teens care about climate change? A recent *Lancet Planetary Health* study showed that climate change takes the forefront in teen worries. Young people believe that we have failed to care for the planet and that the government is not doing enough to protect it.
- **Family Security:** Almost everyone has noticed the gradual shift in family dynamics. We as adults feel it, and the effect has not been lost on our kids. They live in fear of losing the stability they accept. In addition, those

whose parents are going through a challenging phase in their marriages and partnerships are unsure where the chips will fall. So, you can imagine just how agonizing that would be.

- **Failing:** Nobody likes to fail, and your teen is no different. But it seems to be a much bigger concern for Gen Zs. They intend to succeed in everything - academics, social life, career. It might not seem like much of a problem, but it is. When teens think they have failed, the probability of being anxious or depressed only increases.

- **Poverty:** Gen Zs live in the ruins of the recession, with reminders everywhere to drum this into their existence. They see their parents working hard, watch the news on rising living costs, and know that it's hard to live a comfortable life without money. So it's only natural that the possibility of poverty would scare them.

- **The Future:** What is in it? What will they be? Will they achieve their goals? What will life after graduation entail? Teens don't know what lies ahead of them, which scares them. Wouldn't you also be petrified at the thought of walking into the unknown?

- **Safety:** With BLM movements and school shootings splashed across our headlines, our teens are aware of what a scary place this world can be, now more than ever. They need reassurance and a safe space to talk about how they feel about these recent events.

The next time you see your teen lost in their thoughts, know that any of these concerns could cross their mind.

Walking in Your Teenager's Shoes

I offered to take my sixteen-year-old niece to the mall the other day, and it was quite a long ride. She started recording everything we were doing from the get-go, including filling the tank! She even had me strike a pose and wave to her phone while at it -very comical. It felt like I was hanging out with her and the people who live inside her phone–through the shopping experience, lunch, and even the way back home. At some point, we had to wait ten minutes at the mall for her followers to vote on whether she should buy a blue or black dress. They all looked the same to me, the same design, and all. But she needed a vote, so we stood there, watching the votes come in and the percentages changing. As we wandered around the store for those minutes, I finally had a full-on conversation with my niece about the school, career ideas, and hobbies. It was the first time I was talking to just her, then the timer rang, and it was back to her, the phone, and me!

You might wonder why I was so patient with all of this. First, I love my niece, and the opportunity to hang out with her was a welcome one. Then there's the fact that I have a teen and understand just how vital *social currency* is to teenagers. Social media likes and follows constitute the Gen Z rat race. So, what else are Gen Zs thinking about when they are not busy staring at their phones?

- **Their Grades:** Yep, most of these kids still care what they score in school. Now that they understand just how important it is to succeed academically. It might not look like they do, but the stress of their piling assignments gets to them.

- **Their Identity:** Let's forget about gender identity for a moment. Instead, your teen will wonder, "who am I?" As they try to figure this out, you'd best believe someone will try to push some drugs their way. Oh, and fitting in is still an issue. They still have tables marked out for the cool kids, drama geeks, nerds–you know how it goes.

- **Their Bodies:** We had the size two models sprawled all over our magazines growing up. If you thought that was terrible, welcome to the age of Photoshop and filters. Celebrities are now propagating this idea of the perfect body type. They post pictures with lean muscles and bulges just in the right place. Body image is so important that when someone accidentally leaked an unfiltered Khloe Kardashian picture, it was gone by the next day! So, imagine trying to live up to these unbelievable standards.

- **Romantic Interests:** Teens still develop romantic feelings towards each other. So, even if your teen has still not talked to you about a love interest, it could still be a possibility. And let's not forget that it comes with the added pressure to have sex.

- **Trends:** Being fashionable is never going out of style. And with kids wearing designer clothes and showing off on social media, you can bet that your teen might have fancied the idea too. Could it be that the latest fashions also entrance them?

- **Jealousy:** Even among the cool kids, there's still a bit of competition. People want to be the star quarterback or the queen bee who has everyone in awe. So, your kid could be wondering what this person has that they don't.

- **Sexual Orientation:** As your teen starts romanticizing other people, they may realize that they are questioning their sexual orientation. Now would be an excellent time for that talk.

- **FOMO (Fear of Missing Out):** Welcome to the social media era. Back in the day, your friends could go partying, and you would not know about it. But now, they splash the images and videos all over their social pages. So, if your kid must stay in for some reason, they will feel left out.

Whoa! Those are quite many *struggles*:

- Not having much impulse control,
- Facing the reality of the future and feeling lost in all of it, and
- Navigating the social pressures of being a teenager in the social media era.

It's no wonder our teens seem so strung out. Is there anything you can do as a parent to make this journey easier?

Shaping the Teenage Mind

Okay, so you can't buy a developed prefrontal cortex and gift it to your teen (though you probably wish you could)–which means you've got to accept the fact that your teen is still not an adult. You can't expect them to reason like one. But they are not a child either, so you cannot expect them to live in oblivion of their realities. They know that life is changing fast, and it scares them to be present while unsure of what role they play.

How do you balance these two extremes? First, let's see how we can quell their concerns while enabling them to do and be better in this transitional period:

- **Listen:** We are often embroiled in passing on lessons that sometimes we miss the most important things–like listening. Your teen's brain is now teeming with information and ideas. How about you take the time to listen to them? Some ideas will be outrageous, but some will inspire and shock you.
- **Be Patient:** So, your teen talked smack, and you want to ground them for a week. But does that change the fact that their brain is still developing? No! Instead, learn to take a few deep breaths before reacting. Ask yourself,

is this a one-time thing, or do you see a pattern here? Patterns require discipline, while one-off events can do with just a conversation.

- **Set the Rules:** Just because your teen is going through a phase does not mean that you or anyone else needs to withstand it. Clarify that it's not acceptable for your teen to be disrespectful to you or their siblings. Involve them in this decision and let them understand where the boundaries lie.

- **Teach Them:** Is there a way your teen can express their anger or frustration without being nasty? Sure! You just need to point them in that direction. Oh, and practice it too. You can't be asking them to cool off before reacting, yet you walk around like a time bomb, eager to go off at the slightest provocation.

I want to say that the rest of the teen years will be easy, but that would be a blatant lie. The more your teen's brain develops, the more 'out there' ideas they will throw your way. So, you need to understand how to listen to them without judging their genius. They are growing into adults–isn't it time you started listening to them? If you're having a problem navigating back and forth between you and your teen, you will enjoy the next chapter. It talks about what we struggle with when talking to teenagers: communication!

***

Chapter Five

Are You Communicating With Your Teen?

"It's hard to understand exactly what a person means through texting... when you are face to face; you can see their expressions and know exactly what they mean." —Teen

Most parents often talk about what they would change about parenting their teens now that they know better. Some feel they were too harsh, always yelling at their kids, while others were barely present. In my case, it's quite a different case. I thought I had it all figured out because I was not the parent who ordered my kid around or belittled what they were going

71

through. So, I would see these parents cursing at their kids and think, "whoa, if only they knew just how damaging that can be to a child." But I had no idea that I was also going about it the wrong way. I was the advisor. My teen would come to me, and I would be quick with a suggestion, "Oh really? Why don't you do this?" or "You should do this." The whole time they were bearing their heart out to me, I was busy thinking of a solution. "Ah! So, your math teacher insists on two assignments this week. Why don't you start the first one now?" My teen would nod, happy that they had a solution, and I would smirk and pat myself on the back. Job done!

The advice kept on coming, and if anyone had asked me if I was doing an excellent job as a parent, I would have said that I deserved an award. Little did I know I was blocking communication with my teen. All I was doing was sending a message that they did not have what it took to solve their problems. So, they kept coming to me for advice, and I kept dishing it out, and before I knew it, we were in a vicious cycle. They barely even thought of ideas to get out of trouble - they knew I had their back. I was the think tank, and it was only later that I realized how wrong I had been about communication. I had taught my teen that they could handle nothing without me!

While you cannot be breathing fire in your home, you also can't raise teenagers by solving all their problems. You're there as a sounding board, not as the problem solver, and I now know I had it twisted when I started.

Why Communication Matters?

"(Online/texting) gives me more time to think out what I want to say and if I'm scared to ask someone, I might feel more comfortable asking them through those means." –**Teen**

Communication has changed over the years. We barely spoke to our parents when we were not in the house back in my days. We would ring them when we got to our friends' homes, let them know when we would be back, and that would be it. They had no way of keeping tabs on what we were doing. So, when we got home, we would relay what had happened, and they would take our word for it. Unless the police walked you home or rang up your parents, that was a whole other scenario.

But now, keeping track of teens has become much more manageable. They do not have any reason not to communicate. They can text, call, email, or even share their location with you anytime! With this increased connectivity, you would think that connecting with your teen would be a breeze. But it's not. Sure, you may track their phone all day and even hack into their messages, but are you communicating with them? Does knowing where they are and what they are doing help you get closer to your teen? For most parents I've talked to, it's not the case. They connect electronically but are still not on the same page! Why? There's little or no communication, and even when they talk, they hit a wall.

Do you need this two-way street with your child? A resounding yes!

Connecting with Your Child

If you think about it, you barely get to see your child. They are out the door at the first light and come home later in the evening, tired from a long day of after-school activities. They then spend the night scrolling their phone and catching up with homework. So, where does that leave you?–on the sidelines, watching your teen grow faster than you could have imagined. As they master their independence, they pull away, making it harder to know what they are up to. But with open communication in the home, you can still be a part of your independent teen's life. Rather than rely on the crumbs they leave lying around, you can get into the meat of things–who are they hanging out with? What makes them happy? Are they concerned about something?

But here's the thing: teens will only open up about these things when they feel listened to. If they think you will shut them down or shun their emotions, they will bottle up all that information and share it with anyone who listens. You can cross your fingers that the recipient will use that information for good or be the ear on the other side of that conversation.

Building a Friendship

The more your teen tries to establish their independence, the more the need they feel to somehow disengage from you. Their peers' opinions matter more to them -*what should I wear? Do you think I should go on a diet? Should I accept that date?* You might think that your teen has their bases covered now that they have peers facing the same struggles as them. But that does not take away your role as a parent/friend. Your teen still needs to know that you will be there when they need you, when the world has turned against them, or going through something they don't want to share with their peers. If a teen feels safe sharing their fears and interests with you, they will be more prepared to face the world. Besides, it gives you the chance to weigh in on some decisions. Teens may think they have it figured out, but some of their ideas are not the best.

Shaping Your Teen

I'll use a common scenario. Suppose you work with a colleague with whom you often lock heads. Assume that this colleague now wants to show you how to do something. Would you be open to hearing their suggestion? How easy would it be to trust that they had pure intentions? It's the same case with your child. You cannot berate them most of the year, then expect them to receive any advice with open arms. You need time to break down any walls they might have put up, and only then can you guide them on the right path. It does not mean that you will always agree, but you are halfway there if you can agree more than you disagree!

Resonating With Your Kid

Are you open about your experiences as a teen? I know talking about how you got drunk and almost set a house on fire does not look like a good idea. *What if your teen gets excited by the concept and recreates the whole thing?* But acting like you never made mistakes puts pressure on your teen to be this perfect person. You can let them know all about your escapades and what you wish you had done differently with open communication. They can then see you as a person and know that they, too, can always change their path if they want to.

In today's digital age, it's even more important to have open discussions with your kid. It gives you a baseline of where your child is at. That way, when they show signs of mental distress, you know you do not imagine things.

Differences Between Talking To and Talking At Your Teen

"Teens are people. Everybody has times when they can't communicate, but it depends on the person, not the age." –Teen

I shared my experience of always advising my teen instead of letting them find their path. I weakened their resolve to come up with solutions, which inevitably put quite a load on my back. Why? Not only was I dealing with my problems, but I also had to solve my teen's. I felt the heft, but thought that bearing this burden was worth it because I protected my child from tough decisions and was there for them at every step. But I was wrong because I sent the wrong message each time I stepped in. So, the load got heavier and heavier until I finally had to let them take up their part. You can imagine how hard it was to undo all those years of picking up the slack on their behalf.

Are you sending the wrong message to your kid? You could be in for quite a journey. Let's see how you might do this and what you can do instead.

Suppose your kid comes to you and says, *"I can't keep up with my maths assignments. The teacher just added more work, and I am barely done with what he wants me to submit tomorrow."*

Reaction 1

Assuming you are an advisor as I was, your reaction would probably be in the line of, *"why don't you first finish tomorrow's submission then work on the next assignment?"*

See what you did there? You solved their problem for them, **communicating** that your child does not have what it takes to solve their problem.

Reaction 2

Another parent might go, "It's going to be okay. Don't worry about it."

Most of us grew up hearing this. It only **communicated** that our feelings were invalid–that we had no right to feel angry, frustrated, or stressed. The result?–Your teen stops opening up about things for fear that they might not be significant enough to warrant a conversation.

Reaction 3

Imagine what your teen would feel if you responded with an "Oh wow! I bet those three assignments must be harder than my 9-5! How about this? I'll go to school, and you can take on my job."

Sarcasm is never the way to communicate with your child. It **communicates** that you do not care about what they are going through because, in your eyes, it is insignificant.

Reaction 4

Some parents get by with changing the subject. Out of nowhere, such a parent could go, *"Let's go grab some pizza."* And even when they get to the pizza place, they still don't address what the teen said. To a teen, this **communicates** that their problem does not matter to the parent.

Reaction 5

Have you ever come across a parent who believes that their teen is often or always in the wrong? To them, a likely answer could be, *"Is the added work because you skipped a test or did not hand in an assignment?"* Then the conversation takes a turn, with the teen forced to defend themselves and point out that they are not to blame. Before long, the teen **understands** they are to blame for whatever happens to them.

Reaction 6

This reaction is like advising. But rather than suggest what the teen should do, you order them, e.g., *"You must first finish tomorrow's assignment, then work on the others."* You communicate that your teen cannot handle their problems like with advising. Only that, in this case, you clarify that you're the one holding the reins in their life.

None of these reactions helps you communicate with your teen. It just sends the wrong message, prompting them to either rely on you for solutions or keep you in the dark about their problems. Take any scenario below and ask yourself how you would handle the situation:

- Someone hacked into my Instagram account and is now impersonating me,
- My friends won't talk to me because I missed a party last week,
- I don't know if I should join the drama club or keep playing football even if I prefer drama.

Are you seeing any similarities between your reaction and the poor communication examples above? What would you do differently now that you know what sends a wrong message?

Is Your Teen Listening To You?

"Although teens rely on the internet for nearly everything, friendships can't survive without seeing someone; this forces people to communicate without a computer." —Teen

You've been pacing the room for almost an hour, going on and on about why sneaking out at odd hours is not acceptable in your home. You've vividly pointed out the dangers of being out at night, why drinking is not a good idea, how worried you were that your teen was in trouble, and why you think your teen needs a new curfew. Then you look at your teen and see this dazed look on their face, almost as if they can't see or hear you. They sit there, probably zoned out and waiting for the big finale. Or worse, they are scrolling their social media, glancing your way from time to time and unbothered by what's happening around them. That right there is a sign that your teen is not listening to you. But are there less obvious signs that your teen is not actively engaging in the conversation?

Of course, there are! Your teen:

- **Interrupts you mid-sentence:** You could be in the middle of a crucial point, but they don't feel the need to wait it out. So, your teen jumps in with their rebuttal as they please.

- **Does not make eye contact:** Rather than focus on you, their eyes dart across the room, over their phones, across the yard, anywhere but you! Even when you are not talking about sex, they still seem unable to maintain eye contact.

- **Does not ask for clarifications:** You go through the whole conversation, and not even once do they ask you to clarify or repeat a point. It's almost like they understand everything, even when you stumble through the words.

- **Does not exhibit any emotions:** They sit there, still, and with their face unchanging. You talk about emergencies the first time you got a job, when you were caught in a police chase, nothing.

- **Does not acknowledge your emotions:** You could talk about how frustrated you were when they were missing, yet they offer nothing. There's no "*I see where you are coming from*" or "*that sounds scary.*" Nothing.

- **Does not broaden the conversation:** Even when you offer them something they can use to keep the conversation going, they don't take it.

When you are not communicating with your teen, that's precisely what they give you -nothing! And even when they spoke up, it's voicing how misunderstood they feel and how you are frustrating them. Or worse, they don't speak up at all, so you get nothing.

Why Teenagers Rebel Against Authority?

"I feel that the art of talking to someone face to face has decreased, but it is not a total loss." –Teen

It's frustrating to talk to someone who won't talk back to you or only does so aggressively. But could there be a reason your teen won't communicate with you? Might you have something to do with it? Yes, sometimes, our communication barriers are a thing of our doing. Let's see how this works:

Your Teen Needs Time

Let's assume you've had a long day at work, and you walk into the house. Your teen comes running and immediately starts talking about something they need or want. What's the first thing most parents do? They ask for time. *Hey, let me speak to you once I've had a nap. Or I'll put my bag down and then we can talk.* It's the least they can afford you–time. So, why should it be any different with your teen? They also need time to prepare for conversations. Suppose you found your child's Finsta (fake Instagram). Do you go all-in when you see them? Or should you go, "*Hey, I found your actual account on Instagram and would like to talk to you about it. What time is good for you?*" You might think that this gives them enough time to come up with a good lie (which it does), but it also **communicates** respect. Your teen feels like they have control over the conversation and will walk in feeling more level-headed. You will have an easier time communicating with them when they don't feel attacked.

You Do Not Listen

Do you remember when we went through several reactions that sent the wrong messages to teens? Suppose you've been using any of those reactions. You will have barely scratched the surface because each time your teen communicates their feelings, you either disregard them or solve their problems for them. But what if you took the time to dig a little deeper? Then you would have some pointers and know where they are coming from. For example, your teen has been struggling with assignments and seems irritable. You can start with reflections: *"You have a lot of schoolwork right now and are having a hard time managing your schedule. Could this be why you seem irritable lately?"* Your teen will see that you are trying to reflect on their situation, making them feel heard. The result?–They will be more open to talking about it.

As much as reflection opens up communication, do not assume things. Always come from the point of understanding. If you do not know what's happening, then seek to understand what's happening.

Your Teen is Angry

I'd be lying if I said that effective communication makes everything hanky dory. It does not. Sometimes, you and your teen will be angry at each other, and things can get out of hand. It's not uncommon for teens to slam their doors at yelling parents. So, assuming your last conversation went left, how can you open that door of communication again?

First, you need to give your teen time to cool off as you catch your breath. Then, set some rules for the conversation, accepting where you could also have gone wrong. Here's an example, *"When we last spoke, our conversation did not go so well, and we did not reach a consensus. I want to propose another way to broach the subject to avoid that outcome. How about we use a talking stick? When you're holding the stick, you talk, and vice versa, and we will not interrupt each other."* You can always find something that can work for your teen to ensure they feel heard.

When your teen feels respected and knows that their opinion matters, they voice their concerns more. They will not share everything with you, but they will open up more than before.

How To Get Your Teen to Listen to You

"People aren't used to talking in person, how to respond to things on their toes, without having a computer to hide behind." –Teen

Getting your teen to listen to you is easy. Do you see patterns in how you communicate with your child? Teens want you to:

- **Remain Calm:** Have you ever walked into a conversation ready to react when things don't go your way? That does not work with teens. Even if they respond aggressively and start becoming loud, do not raise your voice. The less emotional you are, the more grip you will have on the situation.

- **Be Respectful:** We always demand respect from our kids, but do we give them the same treatment? You want your teen to respect your time, but you will not respect theirs. You want your teen to listen to what you say, but you will not acknowledge their opinions. Respect, just like communication, is two-way.

- **Withhold Judgment:** So, you find your teen doing something wrong, and the first thing you do is lash out at them. It makes them feel judged, and they can hide away in shame or become even more defiant. Some teens will want to justify what they are doing, making communication harder. How about taking a step back and leaving judgment at the door?

Learn to listen to your teenager. We often stress telling them what to do that we forget that they have a say in all of this. Say you want to impose a curfew. What does your teen have to say? You might disagree with them, but at least they will know that you listened to what they wanted to say. It makes a lot of difference.

The question is, are you listening to your kid? Let's find out!

Are You Hearing or Listening to Your Teen? What's the Difference?

"You act differently around different groups and people. My online pages are who I am around my friends. I will not create a page based on the personality I have around my parents, but the personality I have around everyone else." —Teen

The other day, I grabbed lunch with a friend, and the restaurant owner came over to chat. We were talking about stock options, and she intended to make us see things her way. I had already decided that I would not invest in the said stocks, and so had my friend. But she went on and on about it, despite both of us being clear that we had another preference. Eventually, she asked me, "Are you with me?" I had already checked out of the conversation and was whiling the time away, so I answered her with an "I hear you." To which she replied, "You hear me, but are you listening?" Of course, that woke me up from the food coma that was traversing my system. "What an important observation," I thought to myself. She had gathered that I was not taking in the information by hearing her because I was not processing it as I should have. She was right, because I did not even look up the said stock after leaving the restaurant.

It's easy for someone to hear you and not pay a second thought to what you have said. Could this be what's happening to you? How can you tell that you are not listening to your teen?

- **Your Teen Shows Signs of Frustration**: How would you feel if your opinions fell on deaf ears? Your teen is now becoming an adult, which means they crave more independence. They want a say in some rules, so they will feel frustrated if you won't bend just a little. They act out by slamming doors, screaming, and staying out late.

- **Your Teen Has A New Group Of Friends**: When you pay attention to your kid, you know who they are hanging out with. So, if they socialize with a new group, you will understand why. Maybe they have issues with their other friends or have joined a new club. But if you have no background information on this change, then it's a sign you're not listening to your kid. What's happening in your child's life?

- **Your Teen Seems to struggle with Weight**: Most teens go through a phase where they eat a lot or seem interested in being fit. But drastic weight changes are often a sign that something is not right. Maybe your child is having a rough time at school, being anxious, or dealing with an eating disorder. Sometimes, it can be a medical condition. But in most cases, it points to a mental struggle. When you have open communication with your kid, you can know more about what's causing this change. The same goes for drastic academic changes.

- **Your Teen Does Not Share Much**: Would you be open to talking to someone who disregards you or shuts you down? Neither is your teen. So, if they have somehow reduced the amount of information they share with you, it's a sign that they are not feeling heard.

So, what can you do about it?–become a better listener!

Tips on Becoming a Better Listener

*"It's not that I put anything bad on it, but them checking up is a sign of distrust." –**Teen on social media***

I was the parent who could not just listen to my teen sharing a problem. Instead, I would be on the edge of my seat, eager to offer a solution and show just how helpful I was. I was failing to be a good listener. Do you know what I should have done instead?

- **Listening**: We are often engrossed in the whole back and forth that we miss the most crucial part -listening. Just sitting there, nodding and smiling -a sign that we hear the other person and understand what they have to say. That might be all your teen needs; a listening ear. Sometimes, your teen does not need resolution. They just want a safe space to be honest with what they are feeling.
- **Being Attentive**: Avoid fiddling with your phone or getting lost in your thoughts as your teen talks. Sure, they may talk about why vampires were so last decade and why Marvel movies are the real deal. But that's

what they are interested in -so engage all your senses in this.

- **Using Open Body Language**: So, your teen comes to you about their dating life. And you sit there, arms crossed, pensive, with your body straight and eyes narrowed. What does this communicate?–You are not open to discussing the subject. Instead, show interest by leaning forward, relaxing your muscles, and smiling reassuringly. Open that door.

- **Not Interrupting Your Teen**: Interruption kills a conversation. Your teen might be mid-sentence talking about why they want to lose weight by summer. Then you hold up your finger, interrupting them rudely and triggering anxiety in them. Oh, and it also screams disrespect -like hold that thought, I have something more important to say! So, your teen finishes their thought fast, feeling unheard.

- **Posing Questions**: There's a difference between rudely interjecting as your teen speaks and asking questions. Wait for the right moment and ask for something. "What did you like the most about your trip?" "Did you have fun last night?" "How does that make you feel?"

Questions signify an interest in the topic and enhance the conversation.

- **Maintaining Eye Contact**: No matter how mundane the conversation seems, don't avoid eye contact. Maintaining this connection shows that you are keen on the conversation.

Now that you have mastered communicating with your teen, what's next? You'll need to keep that door open as we head towards the murky waters of sex, dating, and drugs. So, remember what your teen confides in you and follow up with them. For example, if they want to decide if they will join a club, ask them how it's going. It shows that you care beyond the conversation. Keep it between the two of you. So, your teen likes someone and tells you all about it. Should you embarrass them by telling everyone? No! But you should always seek help if the confession shows that your teen could harm themselves or others.

***

Chapter Six

Boundaries vs. Walls: Navigating Parent-Teen Relationships

"If you have never been hated by your child, you have never been a parent." –**Bette Davis**

When my child was young and still believed in Santa Claus, I often pondered their teen years. Would we still cuddle when reading bedtime stories till they nodded off with a relaxed smile on their face? Of course not! But would they still look up at me with this wondrous look, one that melted my heart and welled up in my eyes? Would they still share their dreams with me?

Would we still be *friends*? I envied parents and teens who could crack each other up, somehow blurring the line between parent and child -the parents and teens who would spend time together; camping, shopping, and even taking long walks together. Because growing up, this had not been the case. Sure, we would enjoy time together, but it was always clear that one of us wielded power.

Part of me wanted to change this dynamic without losing my authority. So, when it finally was my turn -would my teen befriend me?

Why Can't You Always Be the Cool Parent?

"It is easier to build strong children than to repair broken men." –Frederick Douglass

Can parents and teenagers be friends? That's a hard one. I could ask ten parents, yet none would give me the same answer. We are all reading from a different script. But here's one thing that resonated with me as I geared up to be a teen parent. Friendship implies equality. Here's an example:

Suppose your fourteen-year-old meets someone on Instagram and decides they would like to meet this individual in person. Heck, they are even okay with planning a getaway in a room with a jacuzzi. Oh, and this other individual is a whopping Thirty-one! So, as a parent, do you go, "Oh, how nice! Send me the deets!" or do you go, "Not in my house you won't!"

Now, imagine your friend has met someone on Instagram and has planned the same getaway. Sure, you could be against it and give an opinion about why you think it's a bad idea. But as a friend, all you can do is weigh in on the situation. You cannot put your foot down and keep them from doing as they please.

So, can you *truly* be friends with your teenager? It gets you thinking, does it not? Being friends with your teen might look like a good idea, but it's not feasible when it comes down to it. I learned the hard way. I would try to be all buddy-buddy with my kid, and when it was good, we were great. We would be that parent and teen high-fiving in the corner and having a good old time. But it would turn into a mess when I kept them from doing something. The thing is, I could not avoid being a parent. *Was I to let my child leave in the middle of the night to attend some party in who knows where? Should I have allowed them to sleep in because they didn't feel like going to school that day? Or was it right for me to pay for their fake ID?* No, in all these instances, I had to be the parent. I had to remind them we were not equal, and that I was the one who stipulated the rules. And then, just like that, I'd no longer be the cool parent–my crown was gone, but at least my child was still in line.

Often, I questioned why I felt the need to be my child's friend. Why did it matter so much to me? Well, people fall into this trap for many reasons. You need to ask yourself:

- **Are you looking for your child's approval?** So, you might try harder to get your child to like you, especially in their teen years, that you are bending over backward for them.

- **Does your child provide some sense of intimacy that you don't get from other people?** Maybe you're having a hard time at work or facing struggles with your partner. Or perhaps you have little of a life outside of parenting.

Some people slowly dig themselves into this whole parent-teen friendship hole without knowing it. Maybe you confided to your child once about your work, and it felt good. She seemed interested, and you took it from there, divulging more about your life and connecting with her on it. But does it work? Unfortunately, no! Studies show that involving our kids in our psychological distress does not help them grow closer to us. It only stresses them. Knowing that you harbor hatred towards your partner, your child only gives them one more thing to worry about — robbing them of their childhood. Does that mean we should lie to them about what's happening in our lives? No, but we should only share what they *need* to know.

Do you want to know why being *friends with your teen* does not work? When children and parents are friends, the boundaries get blurry. It confuses them. So:

- **The teen lives in a home with minimal or no structure.** As a result, they don't need to push themselves to do better in school or even after-school activities. After all, they live in a household where they are free to do what they want. Those in structured homes are high achievers and are less likely to have behavioral issues.

- **The teen does not take well to discipline.** Assume you've let your child run free as they please. Then, one day, you decide you will not allow them to do something. What do you expect them to do?–react poorly to the authority! This bit of discipline will be too much for them to take because they are not used to being under anyone's control. And if they can't take a bit of discipline from you, imagine how hard it will be for them to be accountable in the real world.

- **You feel out of depth.** If you don't have the power to keep your child from doing as they please, you can feel lost in all of it. It's tough for a parent to be happy in such a situation where they feel they no longer have a say. As much as we want to be friends with our kids, we crave that control over them.

Is there a way to be *friendly* with your child without losing your authority? Yes, it's called *enforcing boundaries* in your home. Being empathetic and warm towards your child enables you to maintain as close a relationship as you can with them without losing control. So, let's figure out how you can do this:

How You Can Set Boundaries with Your Kids

"One thing I had learned from watching chimpanzees with their infants is that having a child should be fun." –Jane Goodall

Some people have a hard time with boundaries, mainly because they do not understand them. I remember an instance where I asked a friend to respect my boundary. I felt they were crossing it so much that I was no longer comfortable. They replied, "Alright, I will stay within my boundary." I cracked up at it, knowing that they had interpreted my need for a boundary as punishment to them. Unfortunately, this can happen when you mean well, even between you and your teenager. So, before the concept of boundaries scares you off, let's consider its importance. Why do we need boundaries with our teens?

- They set the rules for what's acceptable on your part and theirs.
- They communicate you care about them by clarifying what they should do in and out of your presence.
- They protect your child.
- They set the pace for making the right decisions.
- They allow them the freedom to decide within the provided structures.

How do you suggest boundaries to your teen? It's mostly about empathizing with them when stepping in as a parent. You should:

- **Be clear on why you enforce boundaries:** Involve everyone in the conversation rather than dictating what you have decided for the household. Talk about which boundaries are important to everyone, e.g.; your teen must be home by six pm every day. Then venture into consequences if the boundaries are not honored, e.g., your teen will lose their driving privileges if they don't comply with the curfew. Also, include the boundaries that have wiggle room. For example, suppose your teen needs to be out past 6 pm. In that case, they can keep their driving privileges by informing you beforehand. Or your teen can enjoy a curfew at 8 pm when they are seventeen. Boundaries can apply to almost anything–sex, drugs, alcohol, social media, parties, friendships, dating, communication strategies, etc. Find the key pain points and ask your teen to contribute to the conversation.

- **Walk in their shoes:** It might be awhile since you were last a teen, but you can recall what it was like. Then, everything was such a big deal–what grades you scored, what your friends thought of you, the car you drove. And, anytime things didn't go right, you wished the earth could swallow you whole. Remember this and try to connect with your child. Statements like "I remember how that felt" show your teen that you are trying to understand them.

- **Pave the way for accountability:** Are you always quick to rescue your child? Maybe it's time you stopped. For example, if your teen wakes up late and realizes they have two assignments to hand in, do you help them lie to the teacher? No, you empathize with them and support them as they gear up to face the consequences. It teaches them to be more responsible, and they will think about that the next time they have assignments due. As a parent, watching them squirm can be heart-wrenching, but they need you to just support them without stepping in.

- **Do as you say:** Teens will always push boundaries to see just how far you can cave. So, if you state they should be home by 5 pm, they will show up minutes later, then half an hour later, and before you know it, they are staying out all night. They will go as far as you let them. So, be clear about the boundaries and if they cross them, let the consequences follow. Don't be a pendulum on this one.

- **Avoid being dictatorial:** Enforcing boundaries is a natural parenting process, but how you do it affects how well your teen responds to them. So, what's the right way to put your foot down? Start by discussing the set boundaries, then ask your teen to identify why their behavior is not in line with this. Next, discuss the best consequence for their actions and follow through with it. Then encourage your child to abide by the boundaries in the future by providing a nurturing environment.

- **Learn to let go:** Your teen will not always want to spend time with you. Sometimes, they will want to skip 'family night' and watch a movie with friends instead. Rather than taking it personally, take a deep breath and allow them to enjoy their individuality. Unless your teen is pushing the boundaries, allow them to be who they are. Boundaries are not prison walls–they are just protection measures.

- **Respect their boundaries:** Your teen also has a right to enforce boundaries. They are now coming into their own and need to know that you recognize it. So, if something is important to them, e.g., knocking before entering their room, please respect it. Do not mock them or laugh at their individuality.

Oh, here's something you should know–boundaries will evolve as your teen grows. They also change depending on your child's behavior. So, be ready to make some changes while explaining to your kids why different rules apply to them. *Why does one child get home at 6 pm while the rest come at 9 pm? Why can your teen attend a party on Halloween night while your seven-year-old must go trick or treating?*

Being clear on why these boundaries exist will ease communication in your home and strengthen that parent-child bond. You might not become their best friend, but they'll know that you are looking out for them -even if sometimes you'll feel like the enemy.

Complaisant vs. Overbearing Parents: Who Wins?

"The best way to make children good is to make them happy." –Oscar Wilde

Have you heard of 'yes' parents? They seldom say no to their kids, which is quite a far cry from what parenting was back in the day. Growing up, I almost expected to hear 'no' each time I asked for something. "Can I...?" "No!" the answer would come, fast and knocking the breath out of me. So, to see the number of 'yes' parents in the world is quite surprising. This form of parenting has some perks–kids grow up believing in themselves, and it takes some work off the parents' backs. Unfortunately, some parents have become so complaisant that they no longer establish rules for their kids. They believe their kids know what's best, and of course, I broke down what this lack of structure does to kids. Oh, and these kids grow up thinking that the world revolves around them and don't know how to handle rejection. Tell such a kid no, and you might have as well shattered their hopes and dreams. And to such parents, laying down the law becomes a foreign concept–they have said yes so much that when they finally say no, all hell breaks loose. They have minimal to no control over their kids.

Then there's the other end of the spectrum–the 'no' parents, also known as control freaks or overbearing parents. They hardly leave any room for their kids to breathe. From the minute their kids are up, these parents are already breathing down their necks. "Get into the shower. Where are your socks? Have you finished your assignment? Here's a correction–do it now." It's a lot of green and red lights, with the parents dictating what the child *should* and *should not* do. So, what happens to such teens? On the upside, they have so much structure in their lives that they barely have time to entertain other ideas. It does not mean these teens won't do drugs or get into inappropriate relationships. Still, they are less likely to do so. Oh, and they are often high achievers with no option but to excel or face the wrath of their parents. And on the downside? Well, they rebel! They want the freedom to make their decisions, yet their parents are ever backing them into a corner. So, they act out, grasping at the chance to have a say finally. And the parent ends up feeling frustrated.

Both extreme parenting styles have shortcomings for the parents and teens. They both end up frustrated, with the other feeling unfulfilled in their role. So, can you balance the two? Yes, here's how:

- Figure out what you have been doing so far. Have you been a passive parent, sitting back and watching your kid come into their own? Or have you been all up in their business?
- Next, figure out the best structure for your kid. Do you want to enforce more rules in the home, or do you want to give your kid a bit more freedom? Here's where the boundaries will come in handy.
- Prepare for a reaction from your teen. You can't be the parent who follows their child's every move only to sit back all of a sudden. Your kid would think you are

trapping them or punishing them for some reason. Instead, communicate to your child that you change how you do things and explain why. That way, they feel safer in the home.

Boundaries, boundaries, and boundaries – these will help you enforce structure in the home and ease communication between you and your kid.

Does Your Teenager Need Space?

"Most things are good, and they are the strongest things, but there are evil things too, and you are not doing a child a favor by trying to shield him from reality. The important thing is to teach a child that good can always triumph over evil." –Walt Disney

You're in the middle of an argument, and your teen runs up to their room and slams it shut. What do you do?–Follow them and barge in demanding an answer? Or do you wait for them to cool off and talk to them about it later? The correct answer is to wait. Teenagers need their space as much as we do. Why?

- **They need their privacy:** Now that they are becoming adults, they need to have space. It allows them time to be who they are, catch up with friends, explore their desires, and do other things they would instead not share with you. By invading their privacy, you communicate a lack of respect that does not align with your set boundaries.

- **They want to assert their independence:** Teens get to a point where they do not need you around as much. So, they become more comfortable doing their homework by themselves, ironing their clothes, and even spending more time away from you. They do not want you hovering around, spying on them, and creeping them out. And if you do this, you reduce their independence, creating a dependency that will probably outlast their teen years.

- **They want to feel trusted:** What happens when you insist on constantly invading your teen's privacy? Maybe you casually walk in and ask what they are doing, who they are talking to, or why they are in the room alone. What are you doing?–Communicating that you do not trust them.

Your teen will need privacy from time to time, and that's normal–it does not mean that they are doing drugs or linking up with strangers on the internet. They are just growing into who they are. So, learn to separate the need for privacy from bad behavior. Besides, use the communication strategies we discussed in the last chapter. You will have an inkling of what's happening behind closed doors.

Does that mean you should be hands-off with teen privacy? Well, there are exceptions. If you notice your teen:

- Sleeps almost all day,
- Has withdrawn from their favorite hobbies,
- Seems to use substances,
- Has suddenly lost or gained a lot of weight, or
- Is not doing well in school.

It's time to ask your teen if all is well. Is anything the matter? With open communication, you can get down to the meat of things and help them out instead of pushing them away by crossing their boundaries.

Will you ever be *friends with your child*? Once my teen was no longer in the tricky teen years, I thought we would become fast buddies. But it turns out that parents and kids seldom become friends. Sure, we laugh and enjoy each other's company, but we are still not friends. I am more of a consultant in their life because if I ever blur that line, we will butt heads. And why ruin the perfection that exists presently?

***

Chapter Seven

So, Your Teen Is Dating.
What Now?

"Roughly 1.5 million high school boys and girls in the US admit to being intentionally hit or physically harmed by someone they have been romantically involved with the last year." —CDC

"**H**e ghosted me!" she shouted as she came rushing through the glass doors, heaving and wild-eyed, with an air of urgency around her. I watched the young lady move past the desks, and as my friend and I exchanged glances, we knew what she meant. Whoever was on the other side of that text chain had dropped her like a hot potato. My heart sunk for this poor lady as I started realizing just how hard it must be to date in this digital age. Are you parenting a Gen Z? Brace yourself. You have a lot to learn and unlearn as they step into the dating world. And no, you don't have until they are fourteen or fifteen to have that awkward conversation. You can even have it as early as eight or nine–kids these days grow so fast.

So, let me break down what I have gathered so far about dating in the digital age. It's nothing like it was in the twentieth century. It looks like a video game where each character communicates with others using avatars living inside their phones. How does this work? It starts from the get-go. Your teen will probably not approach their love interest face to face even if they are in the same school. Why do that when they can stalk them on all social media apps until they know virtually everything about them?–their hobbies, where they live, where they hang out, their friends, pet peeves, yadda yadda. See those things you would ask for your crush when you finally got them to grab a shake with you at the diner? Well, that information is readily available online. So, our techie kids know just how to find it and figure out if they like this person. The other day, my niece was scrolling through her phone before she went, "Ew, that's so gross, he's so canceled!" It turns out that her crush likes pineapple on pizza, and to her, that's unforgivable. So, rather than wait until the third or fourth date to discover this *wild* fact about him, she saw it on Instagram. It saves her time, I guess! And that's what most kids do.

The question is, what happens when your kid decides they can move past the pineapple with pizza? They do this weird thing where they like their crush's photos months before. I suppose this is akin to smiling at someone or bumping into someone in the school hall. Well, if the crush gets the hint, they slide into your child's DMs or start liking their pictures too. It's a whole thing, a wildly perplexing process, but it works for them. Eventually, they chat each other up if the feeling is mutual and one thing leads to the other. Soon, they talk baby names (just kidding). No, the next phase comes down to if they are down to define the relationship and the whole shebang. Mind you. They are yet to meet IRL (in real life) this entire time. So, your kid could be in a whole relationship with someone they have never talked to physically! If they are lucky, they get to have an actual relationship with this other person, meeting in real life and all.

But that's never a guarantee with Gen Zs. So, the entire relationship could be all about sexting and video chats until it runs its course. Now, this end was simple in our days — you would call it quits, and that would be it. But teens nowadays are a bit more complex. They can bench the other person, leave them on read, submarine them, or ghost them. Whoa! I know those are tons of terms, and I would get into all of them, but even if I did, they would likely be outdated by the time this book was out. Teens unceremoniously dump each other. So, they go missing, start giving lame excuses for not communicating, or come and go as they please. It's almost as if they don't know how to say they are no longer invested in the relationship. But you can imagine that if your teen is on the receiving end of this, it can be very devastating to them. Nobody likes rejection. Then they go through the whole moping phase and start looking for what else is out there.

And if the relationship works, they are cuffed–pretty much signifying that they are lifers doomed to stay together through thick and thin. How romantic. Ah! That pretty much sums up the Gen Z dating scene. Questions?

Is Your Teenager Ready to Date?

"Teens who suffer from dating abuse are subject to long-term consequences like alcoholism, eating

disorders, promiscuity, thoughts of suicide, and violent behavior." —**CDC**

With the fast-paced dating scene at this age, I understand any parent who's on the fence about allowing their kid to date. After all, how can you keep tabs on an avatar? How do you monitor a kid who lives inside your teen's phone? It's all very different from what we were used to in our times. But when you think about it, dating has constantly been evolving. Even for our parents, I am sure the concept of having us walk out the door to watch movies with our dates must have been scary. I mean, how were they to know that we would be where we said we were? In their day, courting was a whole different scenario. So, we can't deny our children the chance to experience dating in this era.

"One in three young people will be in an abusive or unhealthy relationship." –**CDC**

Even as we try to walk on this new journey with our teens, we can't help but feel scared. The CDC released some shocking statistics on teen dating violence that had me shook to the core. Look at those stats -one in every three teens will end up in an unhealthy or abusive relationship. The probability that your teen could be a victim is high.

With that ringing in your mind, you might even feel the need to keep them from ever exploring their romantic feelings. But you can't. All you can do is to prepare them for the dating world, equipping them with the right tools to be safe.

So, where do you start?

- **Understand the signs:** When teen hormones course through your child's body, there's nothing you can do to stop them. You notice they are now keeping more friends, are hanging out in packs, and are almost always chatting with people they like. You might even see signs they are questioning their sexual preference.

- **Listen to your child:** Sometimes, the signs may miss you. But your child coming up to you and stating that they think they are ready to date is a clear sign, don't you think so?

So, if you notice such signs, don't freak out. If you think about it, dating is a fantastic experience. It helps your child sift through what they want and don't want in their future partners. Of course, some people are lucky and find the right partner on the first try. But for most people, it takes several attempts to get it right. So, if your child wants to know what dating entails, then afford them the experience. But wait, not just yet. Wanting to date and being ready to date are two different things.

To prepare your child, get to know:

- **Why does your teen want to date?** Is it because they are interested in someone or feel the pressure to date? Kids are now dating at an early age, which could prompt your child to feel left out. If it's because of FOMO (the fear of missing out), then dating is not the answer. Instead, assure them that waiting a while longer is okay.

- **Does your teen know who they are?** Unfortunately, some people get so lost in their significant other that they barely know how to function when a relationship ends. To avoid this, ask your teen if they understand what makes them unique–their hobbies, goals, etc. That way, they can avoid getting wrapped up in someone else's dreams.

- **What are they looking for in a significant other?** Are there any qualities that stand out to them? What matters to them? Allow them to be as detailed as possible to see where their head is.

- **Do they have a sexual preference?** Does your teen know what they like, or will they use dating as a chance to explore? Now might be the opportune moment to understand if your teen struggles with romantic interests. Also, don't make assumptions about what your child wants. They may have a more challenging time sharing their struggles with you if you do.

- **Does your teen understand boundaries?** We already discussed boundaries in parenting, which will also come in handy here. But how about boundaries with their significant other? Do they know where to draw the line regarding emotional, physical, and sexual interactions? Go through different scenarios with your child. E.g., *Your boyfriend gets mad at you because you won't say you love him back. As a result, he threatens to break up with you. What do you do?* It might feel awkward at first, but it will help your child know how to handle different situations. It also arms them with confidence when putting their foot on the ground.

- **Are there any communication barriers between you and your teen?** As discussed in chapter five, open lines of communication enable you to keep tabs on your teen. But if you have communication breakdowns, allowing your teen to date is a recipe for disaster. If they can't let you in on what they are doing with friends, imagine how hard it would be to know what's happening in their dating life.

- **Is your child doing okay?** Dating in the digital age is even more complex than it was for us. Teens get judged at face value -what they wear, look like, etc. So, a teen who's struggling with body image and mental issues could have it rough navigating the whole ghosting and submerging in the dating scene. Can your teen handle rejection? Do they care about others' opinions? It's better to hold your teen back from dating as you work on developing their confidence than throwing them to the wolves.

- **Is your teen keen on boundaries?** Do you remember the boundaries we set in chapter six? Has your teen followed through on their part? If you are having a hard time enforcing these rules, now is not the best time for your teen to date. Until they can respect the rules, allowing them to date would only worsen the situation.

- Does your teen understand the concept of violence in dating?

- Does your teen understand what's acceptable in your family?

I have discussed the last two points at length later in this chapter.

As you go through each of these questions, which will probably take over one discussion, you will be better poised to gauge if they are ready. Please be objective about it. Don't hold them back based on your fears, yet your child exhibits readiness to enter these murky waters.

Discussing Family Values with Your Teen

"Thirty-three percent of adolescents in America are victims of sexual, physical, verbal, or emotional dating abuse." —CDC

"But Jack's parents let him do…," the list would go on and on, and I would sit there, ready with my answer, "Jack's family has different rules." Of course, this would receive a scoff, an eye roll, or a groan, just something to remind me I was the uncool parent. But that was okay. I had long realized that we all had different parenting styles, even within my group of friends. So, even as my teen started dating, I knew I would face questions about why X got to do this, yet my child could not. Do you know how to avoid these questions when your teen starts dating?–by discussing family values with your teen. What do you expect of your child? Even before your teen shows interest in dating, cover:

When They Can Date

When are you comfortable allowing your child to see a significant other? Here are some examples I have come across:

- **Age Basis:** You can decide that your child is free to date when they hit a particular milestone, e.g., as soon as they are fifteen, they can start dating.
- **A Level Basis:** Some parents are more comfortable with a trickle option, e.g., the teen can start group dates at fifteen, and when they are sixteen, they can start going on solo dates.
- **A Trust Basis:** You can decide that your teen can only start dating when you think they are ready to date. For example, a teen who respects boundaries, communicates effectively, and shows readiness to date would be an ideal candidate.

Each family sets its guidelines based on what the parents believe. For example, some parents feel that early dating is not healthy. Others are for it. Whichever way you lean, it's always advisable to involve the teens, as this is a decision about their lives.

Who They Can Date

Do you have restrictions on who your teen can date? Before you shake your head, consider a thirty-year-old asking your twelve-year-old out for ice cream. Now, do you have any qualms? Okay, maybe that's too out there. But do you have any requirements for the people on your teen dates? Are there any values you'd like to see in them? Here are a few suggestions when vetting the people your teen brings home. Are they:

- Kind? (Generous, compassionate, empathetic)
- People of integrity?
- Responsible?
- Respectful?
- Honest?

Teach your teen how to gauge if a person meets the threshold of your family values. Teach your teen how to embrace these values and walk the talk. For example, they cannot demand respect without giving it. Or expect to attract a kind partner with a self-centered attitude.

How They Should Communicate

Dating in the digital age comes with heavy device usage. But just how much should your teen be on their phone? Are you okay with them texting and calling their significant other all day? You need to discuss:

- If there are any time limits on phone usage,
- What you consider acceptable in communication, i.e., the boundaries your teen should not cross,
- How your teen can use social media to communicate with their significant other,
- How open your teen should be about their phone usage, and
- Where do you stand on sending nudes and nude video chats?

These values barely scratch the surface of what you need to discuss with your teen. But you get the gist that you are only setting the rules that your teen should follow so you can avoid having unnecessary quarrels in the future. Oh, and if you are single-handedly raising your teen, know that your dating life will impact theirs. Try as you might to avoid this interconnection.

How Your Relationships Shape Your Teen's Romantic Escapades

"Violent behavior often begins between sixth and twelfth grade. Seventy-two percent of thirteen- and fourteen-year-olds are 'dating.'" –**CDC**

I barely thought much about how my dating life as a single parent affected my teen until he started dating. It was then that I realized I had unknowingly influenced my teen on what was acceptable. One night, I was in my study and could hear that he and his girlfriend were having a major fight about something. I listened to their voices getting louder, and as I walked over to see what was happening, I heard him say, "We've both had a long day and might say things we don't mean. How about I take you home, and we can discuss this tomorrow?" Moments later, I heard his car engine rev, and I knew they had swept the matter under the rug for now. That was something I often did when I was dating–delaying arguments to avoid saying harsh things in the heat of the moment. And that night, I realized just how much more careful I had to be with what I said around my kid.

Do parents' relationships *really* affect teens' dating lives that much? Oh yes!

- **We model what a normal relationship looks like.** Teens who come from homes where the parents engage in PDA often find that behavior okay. But those who grow up in homes where emotional openness is shunned often have a hard time displaying the same. So, if you think about how you express love to your partner, you might realize it borrows a lot from what you grew up seeing.

- **Teens learn how to handle emotions from what they see in their parents.** For example, suppose your partner opens up to you, and you criticize them for it; your kids will see it. So, they figure they are safer bottling up their emotions, hiding what they feel from their partners. How are you handling your feelings at home? Are you passive-aggressive about it? Are you open about your feelings?

- **Conflict resolution also follows a pattern.** This can go either way. Teens can grow up seeing their parents arguing constantly and even physically fighting. Rather than seeing this as toxicity, they could normalize it and end up as abusers or victims in their relationships. Or they could grow up never seeing their parents argue and think that arguing ruins relationships. Such kids would then walk on eggshells just to avoid rocking the boat. But, of course, that is not effective because they are not true to what they feel.

While it might not be easy to admit, our relationships affect our teens' dating lives, which could be positively or negatively. So, while you might have let some things slide in the past, now might be the time to assess what message you are sending to your kids. They will normalize what you portray as acceptable– so, what's it going to be?

Meeting the Other Parents: Is it Still a Thing?

"Eight States in the U.S. do not consider a violent dating relationship domestic abuse. Therefore, adolescents, teens, and twenty -some things cannot apply for a restraining order for protection from the abuser." –CDC

It's only natural that you will meet your teen's significant other. But should you get together with the other teen's parents? I've heard many arguments about this debate, but we can all agree that we would enjoy some insights into who our teens are dating. Sometimes, meeting the parents is the only way to do that. Why?

- You get to know where the other parents stand on teen dating and inform them of your stance. Are they for teen dating? What have they discussed with their child? What boundaries have they enforced? Have they discussed sex, alcohol, social media, etc.? It might seem unnecessary to go through this, but here's an example of why it's crucial. *I have a friend who was against her daughter having sex until she was eighteen. This young lady (fifteen at the time) was dating a young man (also fifteen) from a more liberal home. So, one thing led to another, and this young couple engaged in sex. Unfortunately, the condom broke, and the two had to source an emergency pill they got from, you guessed it, the boy's parents. Of course, when it came out, it was a huge mess, with the parents at each other's necks.* Could this have gone another way? Who knows? But at least if both parents knew where each family stood, then they could have figured out something. Family values are unique, and what you want for your teen could differ from what the other family thinks is important. Wouldn't you prefer to find out now?

- You get to forge a friendship or at least an understanding with the other parents. It's much harder for your teens to run circles around you when both sets of parents are in on what's happening. Besides, if the parents try to get along, it eases communication between the parents and teens. Plus, the other parents could point out areas of concern you may not have noticed.

Some people might think that meeting the parents is outdated in the digital age, but some things never get old. You need to know who's guiding the young person who's now in your child's life -not so that you can form biases, but so you can do what it takes to protect your family values and your teen.

How You Can Help Your Teen Navigate Relationship Problems

"Only one-third of the teens who were involved in an abusive relationship confided in someone about the violence." –CDC

Parents like being involved in their teens' dating lives–
perhaps to live vicariously through these young souls or
keep tabs on their activities. So, what can you do to help
your teen through the heartbreaks and harsh realities of
dating?

- **Be there:** Sometimes, all you can do is to be there for
  them. You can't keep up with all the platforms and the
  new ways teens have mastered to dump or approach
  each other. So, just accept your role as the parent. Listen
  to them when they come to you, keep an open mind, and
  avoid any communication blocks we covered in chapter
  five.

- **Give your teen space:** Your teen won't be eager to tell
  you that someone ghosted them or ignored their DMs.
  Sometimes, they need to process rejection and hurt in
  silence. Let them.

- **Educate your teen:** The later chapters in this book will
  focus on sex, drugs, social media, mental problems, and
  more. Now is the time to broach these conversations
  with your teen. Are they being careful? Do they feel the
  pressure to send nudes or have sex? Are they feeling left
  out? What can they do about it? You don't want them

learning about these things from their peers or, worse, the internet!

- **Equip your teen with life skills:** Sure, sliding into someone's DMs looks cool. But how great would it be if your teen walked up to their love interest and developed a genuine connection with them or broke up with someone in person rather than submerging them? Teach your child to be respectful towards their love interest and even those who show an interest in them. Just because we live in the digital age does not mean that etiquette does not have a role in our society.

Is there more you can do? Unfortunately, this is as far as you go. All you can do is hope that you have taught your teen the value of a respectful and love-filled relationship where they can thrive. And teach them that if it's not working, they can always walk away, and you'll be there for them.

What if You Don't Like Your Teen's Partner?

We would all like to think that our teens will make the right decision when choosing a romantic partner. But what if you don't like their choice? Here's what you do:

- **Consider why you feel some type of way about their partner.** Are you letting your biases get in the way? Maybe you have prejudged their partner based on your expectations. Is your dislike objective or subjective?

- **Get to know what your teen likes about their partner.** What makes them happy about the relationship? What does their partner enjoy doing? Is there any quality about this person who stands out to them?

- **Allow your teen to be in control.** Your child knows why they chose this person, and unless there is a reason the two should not be together, you need to stand down. Else, your teen can start rebelling, feeling like you are pushing back on their independence.

- **Invite the other teen over.** There's no better way to get to know your teen's partner than by spending time with them. Are they who you think they are? Can you see why your teen likes them? Also, do you like who your child is around them?

- **Focus on the positives.** You will probably be engrossed in picking out what you don't like about your child's partner. Sometimes, we think we are the only ones who know what's best for our kids. But how about you look on the positive side? You could pick out traits that endear your teen to this person.

- **Be respectful.** Even if you have a bias against this person, don't make it obvious. Do not be the parent that stands in the doorway, arms crossed, frowning, and eyeing the kid like a perpetrator. Instead, be open to them as it encourages them to come over more often. Plus, it helps you monitor their behavior from a close distance.

- **Don't resort to threats.** Remember when some parents would threaten to take away their children's privileges if they kept dating so and so? That won't work. It only undoes the hard work we have covered in the past few chapters. Suppose you have genuine concerns about why your child should not keep seeing this person; express them respectfully. Then allow your child the time to digest this information. For example, if you think that your teen's partner berates them, ask your teen how it makes them feel. Then ask them what they think about that behavior, allowing them to realize that they are not being treated right.

Oh, and to help you through this dating phase, keep in mind that most teen relationships don't make it past high school. So, whoever this person is will probably be out of your hair soon. In the meantime, how about you play nice and make them feel welcome?

But what happens if your teen is in an abusive relationship? Do you follow the strategies above?

Addressing Teen Dating Violence (TDV)

"Fifty percent of young people who experience rape or physical or sexual abuse will attempt to commit suicide." –CDC

We sometimes think that violence in relationships only rears its head in adult relationships, but that's not always the case. If the statistics are anything to go by, our kids are exposed to TDV the minute they date. It's time you educated your child on what this looks like–that their partner could abuse them:

- **Physically:** Punching, hitting, kicking, you name it–any physical force used to hurt them.
- **Sexually:** Forcing your teen to engage in sexual activity without their consent–be it oral, vaginal, anal, inappropriate touching, inappropriate wording. Sexual abuse goes further than the physical and includes

sharing explicit content of your teen without their consent. For example, is someone sharing your teen's nudes?

- **Psychologically:** Most states did not even recognize emotional abuse for a long time, but it exists. It's the use of verbal and non-verbal communication to hurt your teen or control them–the use of threats, unkind words, scolding, etc.

And at this age, we must also include stalking. It's common for teens to like pictures of their love interests from ages ago–it's often seen as a sign of interest. But what if it goes beyond this? What if someone continuously sends them DMs and comments on their photos in a way that makes your teen feel unsafe? What if this person threatens your teen or people close to them? It's also a form of abuse that's now rampant with Gen Zs.

What Happens To Teens Who Experience TDV?

Unfortunately, the effects of TDV can last into a teen's adult life and can present in:

- Using drugs,
- Suicidal thoughts,
- Mental health struggles like anxiety and depression,

- Using unnecessary force on other people,
- Tendencies to lie or steal, and
- A higher risk of victimization or violence perpetration in future relationships.

TDV's effects impede a teen's health and hinder them from reaching their full potential. But the problem is that most teens don't recognize when they are being abused. Instead, they normalize name-calling, then incessant teasing, and before they realize it, they have fallen into the hands of a perpetrator. And most of them are afraid to talk about what's happening to them, even with friends and family.

My son has witnessed TDV–not in our home, but his peer group. When he was in his early teens, he made some friends I did not like. And it turns out that my gut feeling was right. These friends were being started into a gang at those early ages. So, they were continuously exposed to older gang members who did not treat women with respect. My son saw just how rough these men were with these young girls. Victims of TDV are highly likely to become victims or perpetrators of relationship-based violence. In my son's case (thankfully), he became a protector. He let go of those friends and made better ones. And he became more mindful of how he treated women and children. I've seen it in the way he treats me with kiddie gloves, how he talks to his siblings, the way he greets neighbors. He's such a warm and fuzzy guy, and we love him for it.

But sometimes, I fear that witnessing the TDV might have also victimized him. In his mid-teens, he dated quite a violent girl. They would argue about something, and she would shove him around. She even slapped him a few times! And broke his phone, scratched him, insulted him, and the list goes on. My son never raised his voice or hands at her, and I am so thankful for that. But he never spoke up for himself. She eventually left him, and to this day, I wonder if he would have left her had she not made this move. I didn't even know what was happening until later, when he talked to me about it.

So, TDV can go both ways. Girls can abuse boys in all ways, and boys can abuse girls. And this experience can be positive or negative. In my son's case, it was both. He became a gentle-natured teen, which was great for those around him–women and children could trust him. But it also weakened his resolve to fight for himself–even now, it's still a work in progress. And it saddens me.

So, how do you protect your child?

- **Educate your teen:** Before your teen starts dating, let them know what healthy relationships look like. *Yes, arguing is okay, but it should not go this far.* Teach them the signs of name-calling, unwanted sexual advances, physical violence, and emotional abuse. Let them know that they should have a say in the relationship and should not feel pressured to do things they are not okay with–and teach them how to get out of bad situations and speak up for themselves. For example, your son argues with his girlfriend, and she slaps him. What should he do?

- **Empower your child:** It's easy to tell your child to stand up when facing abuse. But how about teaching them how to do it? Start imparting assertiveness in them from an early age. It starts with speaking up when the waiter gets their order wrong or when the teacher singles them out, when everyone else is at fault. If they can speak up for themselves in such scenarios, they have a much better chance of protecting themselves.

- **Help them enforce boundaries:** Does your child know the difference between agreeing to something and being manipulated into doing something? Teach them the differences and walk them through why it's dangerous to be a people pleaser. Show them the differences between being kind and ignoring their needs for the benefit of others.

- **Keep the communication open:** Abusers thrive on secrecy. Unfortunately, teens who have a hard time talking to their parents will not know how to tell them they are being abused. Create an environment where your child feels safe talking to you, and if there's ever the need to, they will come to you.

- **Know the warning signs:** Sometimes, the signs are apparent and come as injuries and marks on their skin. But physical changes are not always visible. That's when you need to be warier of changes in weight, grades, motivation, interest in hobbies, mental wellness, etc. For example, a child that was always excited about going to the movies suddenly wants to stay all day indoors, chilling in their room.

- **Don't wait too long to act:** Assuming you've seen that something is not right, talk to your teen. Don't be interrogative. Instead, just ask what's happening in their life. How is school? How is their dating life? If they don't seem comfortable talking about it with you, don't be afraid to refer them to a counselor.

- **Be there:** Your child might be traumatized by the experience and can start lashing out or being moody. Now is the time to show your love and support, rather than judge them for their behavior.
- **Get help:** If you think your teen is in a dangerous situation, get a team on your side. That should include you and at least a school professional. Sometimes, depending on the abuser, you might need to get the police involved.

While it's always best to equip your child to leave the abuser independently, time might not be on their side. So, you might have to step in and nip that relationship in the bud with the help of a professional.

If you thought this subject was heavy, wait till we cover the sex talk in the next chapter!

***

Chapter Eight

The Birds And The Bees: Is Your Teen Having Sex?

"That first time is still some of the best sex I've ever had. I made sure to tell him when something wasn't okay for me." —**Chinwe**

When did you lose your virginity? If we're being honest, we all experienced our virginity loss differently. I had a friend who lost her virginity to her uncle at eleven, one who did it with their boyfriend at fifteen, another who had sex for the first time when she was twenty-one, and one who waited until she was engaged to do the deed. These are but a few of the sex stories I have heard over the years: some sweet, some horrifying, and some downright funny. Mine was a *meh* story, nothing too unique about it -the same old story. A teen makes it to campus, thinks they are in love, falls into bed with someone, sobers up, and realizes sex is not what it's always made out to be.

What have these stories and my experiences taught me? One is that a teen can have sex anytime and at any moment. There's no timeline for it–it just takes two people at the right or wrong place to seal the deal. Maybe there's alcohol involved, pressure, or unending curiosity that pushes your teen to cross that line. So, you can't assume that your teen will follow your path. All you can do is hope that when they finally get to have sex, you will have equipped them with what they need to know to be safe and respectful.

Two is that most of us had sex without fully knowing what it was. I know a friend who was at a party with his brother. The next thing he knows, his brother shoves a condom in his pocket, and that was all the advice he got. So, he went in, fumbled around, and finally figured out what went where. A few minutes later, he was out, and all he got was a pat on the back from big bro. And he was fourteen, having sex with a girl who was seventeen. We often assume that boys are ready to go down that road, but watching him narrate his experience, I could tell that it must have been frightening. And even with all the information available to Gen Zs, sexual experiences are still a murky affair.

We can no longer make do with expecting that our children will wait until they are old enough to have sex. So, we must get involved from the very start–that when they are finally ready, we will be the ones supplying them with the information–not leaving them to fend for themselves in a world full of predators.

What Does Your Teen Know About Sex?

"The first couple of tries were discouraging because his penis would not go in. I felt the ridiculousness of it." **—Deyton**

Awkward moments happen more than I would like, but I would like to share this one, which made me realize how fast kids grow nowadays. We are seated in a café, unwinding after a long day. It's the pre-COVID period, so the tables are pretty close to each other. A couple in their mid-thirties is talking about something they should probably have saved for the bedroom–something about her not having finished the previous night, if you get what I mean.

I can see that my friend is all ears and as the conversation hits a crescendo, we hear a girl squeal from the table behind us. All adults turn to the table, only to see a young girl, maybe ten or twelve, snickering out of control. We're all hoping that she was reading something or watching something on her phone, but no, she was listening to the couple's discussion. Her mom gets up, flustered, throws some notes on the table, and half drags the child from the café, much to our dismay. Just how much do these children know? Well, they know a lot! So, even as you prepare to walk your teen through what sex is, they probably know more than they should at their age. However, that does not mean that you should not have *the talk*.

So, how can you know what your kid knows about sex? And how has this shaped their outlook on the same? First, you walk them through the basics:

What Is Sex?

I know how simple it sounds, but the answer might surprise you. Your kid might think that oral sex does not amount to sex because their understanding of sexual penetration probably boils down to anal and vaginal sex. So, what is sex for your teen?

144

Is Your Teen Having Sex?

Now is the time to find out if your teen has had sex or is having sex.

- Have they had sex?
- What was their experience? Did they like it? Was it consensual? Would they do it again?
- Are they having sex? If so, are they being careful? What kind of sexual activities are they engaging in? How many sexual partners do they have or have they had in the past?

What Can Go Wrong After Having Sex?

The goal is not to scare your teen but to educate them on what could happen to their bodies if they have sex with the wrong person. So, other than teary breakups and awkward silences in the hallway, what else can happen if your teen is not careful when having sex?

- Do they know what STIs are? It turns out that almost half of new STIs are recorded in patients aged fifteen to twenty-four, so those statistics are not in favor of your teen.

- Do they understand that most STIs don't show any symptoms until they ravage the system?
- Have they any clue how people get pregnant? Do they believe in the withdrawal method? What pregnancy prevention methods have they come across, and which ones do they think are effective?

Does Your Teen Know The Effectiveness Of Condoms?

We all know that condoms can break, but does your teen?

- Do they know what to do if a condom breaks?
- Do they know the importance of wrapping up before doing the deed?
- Oh, how about the concept of pre-cum? Does your teen know that this can get someone pregnant too?
- Does your teen know how to use a condom? Do they know how to leave a space at the top to allow for ejaculation?
- Do they know at what time they need to wear the condom?
- Are they familiar with male and female condoms?

How Much Does Your Teen Know About Contraception?

Suppose the condom breaks; what can your teen do to protect themselves or their partner?

- Do they know where they can get an emergency pill? Do they understand the risks of taking the said pill and its effectiveness?
- Have they considered going on the pill? Besides preventing pregnancy, how else can the pill be used in the system?

How Early is Too Early? Is Your Teen Ready to Have Sex?

"I also felt that I was letting down my family. Being raised in a Catholic background, premarital sex is frowned upon." —Rylie

If your teen is not having sex or is yet to cross that line, now is the time to discuss their readiness. Just like dating, there's no timeline for having sex.

- **Are they ready for the emotional reaction that comes from sex?** For example, some people have sex and feel horrible afterward because the other person's response is negative. Can your teen handle this? Are they ready for the emotions they might experience after sharing such intimacy with another person?

- **Have they thought of how they will practice safe sex?** Will they use condoms? Who will buy the condoms? Are they going on the pill? What will they do when something goes wrong?

- **Are they doing it because they want to or no longer want to be the virgin in the group?** Sexual pressure is real and could push your teen to make a life-changing decision on a whim.

Having sex is not just about a physical connection–it also extends to the emotions surrounding the experience. Does your teen understand this? Do they know they could get STIs, get or make someone pregnant, or even suffer emotionally as a result? These are some things they might not learn on the internet–facts they need to hear from you.

Of course, talking about sex with your teen is not easy for you or them. So, before you even venture into it, please go through chapter five and break down any communication barriers you may have. Then, once you are on good talking terms, create a safe and conducive environment where your teen feels comfortable talking to you about their sexual desires.

Also, even with an open door, your teen might still be unwilling to talk to you. Instead, you can refer them to a trusted GP or school counselor to walk them through the basics. They've got to hear it from a reliable source before they start walking the walk.

Sexual Relationships and the Teen

"I ended up trying so hard to "encourage" it. I ended up ejaculating before I'd even put the condom on." –
Tom

Try to keep teens from having sex; studies show that some will still do it. So, how do you talk to your teen about sex?

- **Learn what they know about sex, as we covered above.** Then, please get to know what they think about it, where they get their information, and help them sort the facts from the myths. I have come across so many misconceptions about sex when talking to my teen about his body–sometimes, I just had to take a deep breath and smile my way through it–the internet!

149

- **Create the most suitable environment to talk about sex.** When is your teen most comfortable? Most teens find it hard to look their parents in the eye when discussing condoms and birth control. Or even you, as the parent, might feel some way about it. So, how about you find an environment where you can both thrive? Perhaps on the way to school when it's just you and your teen in the car. Then you can ease your way into it. Or start the conversation after watching a movie together and use the storyline as a foundation for the message. With Gen Zs, you can always use social media platforms and texts to reinforce the communication.

- **Don't make it a one-time thing.** You can't talk to your ten-year-old about sex and expect them to be okay with that information until they are eighteen. Instead, you need to keep reinforcing the message–asking them to be careful when having sex, reminding them that STIs still exist, that pregnancies are natural consequences of sex, etc. If they keep communicating with you about sex, they will be more likely to stay on the right track.

- **Open that door.** Being relaxed when talking to your teen about sex is not easy, and I salute you for trying. But it's the only way that your teen can feel welcome to share their honest opinions about sex–they can sense how tense you are from the minute they walk into the room. So, if you appear unapproachable, they will save their curiosity for their peers or the internet. Does it mean you should fake it? No, you can tell your teen that you are also getting the hang of things. That way, they will understand why you might be uneasy and know that you're open to their questions. Oh, and don't be afraid to admit that you do not have an answer. You can both look for it and learn something.

- **Allow your teen to share.** Sex talks are no longer one-way conversations. Your teen also has a voice to add to this talk -after all, it's their body. So, give them time to express their thoughts, no matter how different they may be from yours. You might see things their way or reach a middle ground. Keep it respectful.

Don't forget to connect your teen to health care providers who can offer medical advice as needed. Sometimes, your teen might not be comfortable talking about a rash they have down there or why they suddenly feel sick in the morning. Allow them the space to deal with it as they work up the courage to open up about it, or not–their choice.

Family Values and the Teenager

"I am seventeen and still a virgin. I've been in situations where it could easily have happened." –
Nemy

Okay, now that your teen is at the helm of their sexual exploration, does that mean that boundaries take a backseat? Not even close. Now is the time to enforce even more family values, ensuring that your teen knows what's acceptable in the household. Talk about these pain points and more, as applicable in your home:

- When are you most comfortable with your teen exploring their sexuality? For example, some parents might decide to put their teens on the pill at sixteen. Others might be more okay with their teens waiting for marriage.
- Do you have any requirements for your teen before they have sex? For instance, do you want them to be in a steady relationship first? Do you want to meet the person they are dating?
- Do you have specifications about where they can have sex?
- Can they have their partners over in their bedrooms?

- Can they have their partners over when no parent is present?

- How do you feel about masturbation? (*We will get into this later.*)

- How do you feel about your teen looking at porn?

- How do you feel about contraception, abortion, condoms, and safe sex?

- Where do you stand on your teen sharing explicit content online or even with their partners?

- What sexual limits would you want your teen to observe?

- Do you have any religious values you want to impart to your teen?

Of course, you and your teen may not agree on these values. So, you need to ensure it feels like a discussion rather than a command. Also, explain the thinking behind your values. For example, why are you, for or against your teen, having sex at fourteen? If your child can understand your reasoning, they are more likely to follow through with your requests. For help with communication, please go through chapter five, and don't hold back on calling a referee to mediate when you have a serious conflict.

Ah and here's a good idea- maybe share your sexual experiences and how they shaped your values. It makes you look human, probably embarrasses your teen, but helps you stick to that landing. But if they cringe and walk away, take the hint.

The Birds and the Bees: When Should You Start Sex Education?

"For our first time, we used a condom. But I had to change it three times because she was dry, and it was painful for her." –Nir

I remember we used to have *The Talk* with our parents back in our day. It was a one-off conversation, and once you had survived those awkward minutes with your parent huffing and puffing through the lines, you were ready– finally free! But now, one conversation is barely enough. Your teen should not be learning about sex during adolescence–you should start them off with facts as soon as they are old enough to understand. Why?

Many kids get sexually abused when they are barely even ten. And when asked to explain what happened to them, they use non-medical terms. For example, a girl once said that a man had touched her monkey. Of course, the doctors were perplexed by what she meant. How did she have a monkey, and what did this strange man want with it? By the time they figured out that she was referring to her vagina, some time had passed. All she knew was that she had a monkey, and it was not ready to eat bananas -such confusing language! Luckily, the doctors found he had not harmed the girl, but what if something had happened?

That's why we cannot delay sex education. But when should we start? Here's a healthy timeline:

- **Ages one to two:** You would think that your kid does not need to know much about sex, but they do. You realize they become more aware of their bodies. So, teach them what they should call their body parts -not monkeys and bananas, but vaginas and penises. Explain the need to be private about their body parts and why they should report anyone who crosses these boundaries. Also, while your child may want to touch themselves, explain the need to do so privately and not in the middle of the food court. Be careful with gender identity at this age–don't start connecting your baby's identity to their sexual organs.

- **Ages two to four:** Most kids start asking where babies come from at this point. Your child will probably care more about the pregnancy than the act that led to their creation. So, talk to them about that and reinforce the need to guard their privacy. Teach them what is acceptable and keep reminding them to come to you if someone crosses the line. Also, ensure they understand boundaries go both ways–they also cannot go around touching people inappropriately. As they explore more of their body parts, explain the role of each part — what does the penis do? Why do girls have different holes for urine and sexual intercourse?

- **Ages five to eight:** The concept of gender identity will probably come up at this point. Please refer to chapter three, where I covered gender roles, identity, and parenting. Besides this, your child will have probably discovered more about their body and will probably explore their desires more. Don't assume that masturbation starts at puberty-sometimes. It begins much earlier. So does sexting and sending nudes. So, talk to your child about how they should take care of themselves online and physically. What should they do when someone asks them for nudes? How about if someone shares explicit content with them? Walk your child through what happens in puberty–how they change emotionally, psychologically, and physically. Is it normal? What can they do to prepare for these changes?

- **Ages nine to twelve:** Kids at this age are now ready to have the actual *sex talk* we have covered in this chapter. Also, walk them through romantic relationships, as we did in the previous chapter. What is acceptable and what is not?

- **Ages thirteen to eighteen:** Your teen may or may not have had sex at this juncture. You can use the insights we covered in this chapter to walk them through safe sex, STIs, pregnancy, abortions, and other core sexual matters. Keep reinforcing the need to maintain a healthy relationship with their partners, as covered in chapter seven, especially for teen dating violence.

Is it necessary to walk through these stages? Yes, and for a straightforward reason -children trust their parents to do what's right for them. So, assuming you talk to your child from an early age about their body, they will feel comfortable talking to you even as they grow older. We all know that teens are secretive. Still, once you have opened this door, they can give you some crumbs here and there to help you help them as they navigate sexual relationships. But what if you have never talked to your child about sex? Well, it's never too late to start!

Masturbation: Getting Comfortable with the Discomfort

"He asked me if I really wanted to do it and that we could wait if I didn't feel ready. He was very sweet."
–Becca

Here's one thing I am happy about–I have never walked in on my teen masturbating, wanking, getting off, whatever you call it. I've never been privy to that part of his life. And I know I'm lucky. Why? Because my friend walked in on their daughter in a compromising situation using a device she didn't even know her daughter owned. The girl was fifteen, and her mother, the poor lady, walked out of the house, took five days off work, and visited her parents. I can only imagine how awkward it was for her daughter, knowing that her mom had caught her in such a position. My advice to her mom was, "how about you knock next time?" But, of course, that was after hours of consoling her on the phone and reassuring her that her daughter was probably going through the same thing–that her daughter needed to hear her mom say that it was okay to explore her sexual desires safely. So, how do you talk about masturbation with your teen?

- **You create the perfect setting:** I keep reiterating the need for a conducive environment because it facilitates effective communication. You can't find your son hurdled in the corner and try to talk to him at that awkward moment. Set a time to speak to them and let them know what you want to cover to prepare.

- **Clarify that they are not in trouble:** Masturbation is often subject to debate, with some people feeling that it's taboo. So, your teen may also think they were wrong to explore their body. So, assure them it's okay and ensure your body language and tone match your words. Only then can your teen feel free.

- **Talk to them about what masturbation is:** Your teen may have already discovered their erogenous zones. Cover what masturbation is, why people do it, and allow your teen to give an opinion. If they are silent, assure them that masturbation is normal, and it's okay to derive pleasure from it.

- **Discuss any myths about masturbation:** Does it weaken their sexual experiences? Will they go blind? Cover all the myths you may have come across and ask your teen about any adverse side effects they may have heard. Also, cover the positive side of masturbation– better sleep, more awareness of their sexual needs, stress relief, etc., -that should be fun!

- **Talk about the need to explore their bodies privately:** While you are not shaming them for pursuing what feels normal, clarify that there's a time and place for this–not during class breaks, not in public, not in front of their video camera, not on Instagram live, etc. Masturbation is a private affair and should be kept.

- **Break down your family values:** What do you believe as a family? For example, you may have spiritual beliefs that don't align with masturbation. Walk your child through these. Let them decide what feels right to them.

Should you share your experiences with masturbating? Some people may feel comfortable letting their kids in on what they did as teens. But don't go there if you are not ready to share this information. Instead, focus on allowing your teen the time to ask as many questions as they would like. If they don't want to discuss masturbation with you, let them know you will be around when they are ready. Don't forget to ask if they need something from you–toys, tissues, lube, etc. If they know, they can come to you for this. They can come to you for contraceptives and other things when sexually active. Not every parent will be comfortable being this liberal with their kid's self-exploration. But ask yourself, *if they don't get these things from you, where will they get them?* Remember that Gen Zs can navigate the internet and find someone willing to sell them what they want.

Oh, and give your teen space. Don't hover around them, barraging them with questions about masturbating. Or walk into their rooms unannounced. But as you provide them with space, don't be like my friend who ran away–they don't need *that* much space!

Teenage Porn Addiction: It's Real

*"He asked if I was ready, and I said yes–I did not even look if he had a condom on or not." –**Siyabonga***

While most people can masturbate by visualizing their sexual desires, others get there by watching porn. There's something such as a healthy amount of porn–you know, the kind that you watch occasionally. Then there's the other end of the spectrum–where you watch porn almost daily and can't seem to do without it. Teens can fall into this trap, and you can tell that they have fallen hard because:

- They somehow no longer are interested in their hobbies and friends and want to remain isolated. And they don't want to talk to you about it because they somehow feel guilty about what they are doing.

- They seem depressed or change their moods often. It's not their doing–porn somehow infiltrates the brain and changes the way your teen feels about themselves. So, feeling depressed soon follows, and you might notice that they are colder towards other people.

- They now want to keep things to themselves more than they did before. Even for a teenager, their level of secrecy feels off. They spend more time in their rooms, in the bathroom, or just staying away from other people. Oh, and a key sign is the guardedness around their devices–they don't want anyone seeing what they are viewing.

- They seem interested in sexually charged language, films, songs, drawings, and other media. When talking with them, you may even notice that they seem to know more than you thought they did.

Of course, these signs could point to something other than porn addiction–your child could face some mental struggles or deal with the usual teenage mood swings. But something is not right if you've noticed an increase in their sexual interests coupled with this secrecy and irritability.

So, how can you help your teen?

- Keep talking to them about sex. Statistics show that talking to your teen about sex enables them to develop a healthy view of sex. Porn illustrates sex as violent and often takes away the notion of consent. I don't want to generalize all porn–some of it is good. However, as kids build up a tolerance to regular porn, it's not unusual for them to watch more graphic content.

- Ensuring you don't enforce any communication blocks, allowing your child to be open with you.

- Coming up with controls over how much your child can access their device to limit their access to porn. With Gen Zs, that means you must stay abreast of social media apps, any new software used in browsing, and any devices that can access the internet.

If you feel you cannot handle the situation yourself, please involve a professional who can help them through it. However, ensure that your child is *actually* struggling with porn addiction before bringing in anyone to help them.

But what if your child shows signs of depression and isolation yet is not busy watching explicit content? In that case, they might struggle with depression, anxiety, and emotional turmoil, as covered in the following chapters. It's worth a read before you call in the experts.

***

Chapter Nine

Depression In Teenagers: Dealing With The Funk

---

*"It was a little of a shock [when my physician
diagnosed me with depression] because I just figured
I was just being sad like any other kid, but I didn't
know it was that bad that I had depression and all
that stuff, and I needed to go on medication." –*
Fourteen-year-old

Joy was a cheerful teenager, fifteen, always ready
with a smile and keen on her education. If she was
not serving in the church or experimenting with lab
chemicals, she was helping at home -you know that typical
carefree teenager who seems to be okay- no issues with

drugs, love triangles, or any of that stuff that keeps parents awake. She had suffered no losses, was doing great in school, had a thriving social life, a family that loved her, and would have to join a great college in a few years. That's not the kid you'd expect to be struggling mentally.

So, it was quite a shocker to her ten-year-old sister when Joy opened up about what she was feeling. They were doing some homework when Joy asked her, "what would you do if I died today?" The younger sister, taken aback by this question, started crying and asked her why she would even ask that question. It was then that Joy realized the gravity of her intentions–unbeknownst to everyone around her, Joy was secretly casing the town for high buildings. She would take the lift to the top floor in each tall building, look at how bad the fall would be if she jumped off, and determine if it was enough to kill her. She wanted to die–and nobody would have been the wiser had she not asked her younger sister about dying. She would probably have chosen a spot and plunged to her death, leaving everyone in shock, wondering why this A student with impeccable manners would decide to end her life. Even she did not know why she wanted to die. All she knew was that she was sad and tired of feeling that way and wanted to put an end to it.

But that's the thing–depression does not affect only those suffering losses and traumas -it can affect anyone. Sure, some people are at more risk than others, but every teenager can fall into this trap. And if we don't know how to spot the signs and pull our kids out of this funk, things can take a wrong turn. So, what happened to Joy? She sought counseling from the school, was put on meds, and seems to do much better–taking this initiative saved her life because this could have turned out differently.

Joy is one example of the many teens who have been through this struggle, some of whom have not been so lucky. Studies show that twenty percent of teens aged between thirteen and eighteen suffer from a mental health condition, one in every five kids. Oh, and the signs show at age fourteen on average. So, your teen's chances of suffering from depression are unfortunately high.

Is Depression Still a Sore Subject?

Depression is very personal to me -it takes me back to my teen years. I was struggling, yet nobody seemed to reach out to help me. I remember feeling lost, unable to do even the simplest of things. Waking up and making my bed took all the energy I had in me–I did not want to do it. I did not want to have breakfast, take the bus to school, or sit through another class. I was tired of it all, and I just wanted to sit in my room doing nothing. I didn't even want to try on new clothes or use the makeup on my dressing table–and to me, that signaled that something was wrong. So, I reached out to my mom, who worked in healthcare. You would think that she would have been sympathetic because she was in the health industry and had come across depression cases before. But she brushed me off, ignored every sign that was right in front of her, and sent me to school. I had no support, and I often thought of putting an end to all of it–yes, I thought about taking my own life.

I was lucky and pushed through high school and eventually made it to college and out of that house. And I sought help. It's been years of therapy, and even now, I still struggle. When I finally had kids, I was wary of passing this depressive state to them. I had to watch how I acted and what I said. I was afraid that the depression was in my genes, and I had somehow passed it on to my children. So, when my son finally got into his teens, I talked to him about depression, what it was, and how it presented. I wanted him to know that he could come to me if he ever felt like he was losing himself. But I did not stop there. I went a step further and watched him like a hawk. *Was he eating enough? Did he have any friends? How did he feel about school?* I hovered, anxious about whether he was doing okay – he never showed any signs of depression. And I am grateful for that.

I know I still must watch over my other kids even before they become teens – and I live with the fear that this depressive state might not skip a generation (I heard that it does that. I've looked for resources to confirm this, but all the sources seem to point to one thing. If anyone in the family has had depression, then there's a high chance that the younger generations will also suffer it.) But of course, it's not written in stone – depression does not only result from the gene pool. Sometimes, it boils down to other factors.

My mother thought I was just a teenager at the time–she would hear none of the talks about being depressed. And over the years, I have come across some other myths that you may also have heard about or believe about depression. They include:

- It's not an actual sickness,
- Only women get it,
- It's just sadness,

- It runs in the family, so if your parents have it, so will you,
- Being on antidepressants changes your personality,
- Once you get on meds, you are never getting off,
- People who talk about being depressed end up feeling more depressed,
- Only people who have suffered trauma can get depressed,
- You can wait out depression, and it will go away on its own,
- Being depressed shows you are weak,
- You cannot heal from depression,
- Depression is imaginary, and
- If you're depressed, you can just snap out of it.

What other myths have you heard? In some cultures, people even believe that if you are depressed, you've been cursed. And yes, I met someone who told me that her aunt, who was depressed, was so because someone put a hex on her. Guess what? The entire family believed it, and because they wanted to be safe, they stayed away from the cursed one.

The other day, I was embroiled in a discussion about whether depression was curable. I insisted it could help someone out of their depressive state with therapy and drugs. Unfortunately, one person in the discussion believed that the person in question was too far gone–that it was too late to help the guy. So, they were content with watching him slip further into the darkness.

These are but a few of the examples I've come across. Even in my case, it took a while before I could share my experience. I felt shame and judged whenever I opened up about it–almost as if I was admitting a great weakness in myself. And I came to realize that I was not alone in it. Most people suffer in silence because they are too afraid of the reactions they get from others when they let them in on this dark cloud. That's why I am vocal about it now–because I am finally in a place of healing, a place that allows me to accept that depression is not my fault. It's not a curse. It's not a sign of weakness. It's not because something terrible happened to me–it's just a result of biological, genetic, and environmental factors. And sometimes, it has no cause! That's just what it is–a mental illness that affects millions of people a year.

Yet, there's so much misinformation about it. So, as much as we have come a long way in exploring mental illnesses, some people are still on the fence about the whole thing. They think that if someone is depressed, something must be wrong with them. Say, for example, that you believe that depression is imaginary. Would you be open to taking your teen to a doctor? You would probably ask them to snap out of it. So, as we start this crucial chapter, I want you to think about your beliefs about depression.

Do you believe it exists?

Would you be willing to explore the options available to your teen if they showed signs of depression?

Is there someone you can talk to who can break down what depression entails?

The sooner you can break these barriers, the easier it will be to walk with your teen on this journey if the need arises. So, is there a way to tell that our kids are battling an internal struggle? Can we save them before they look for a way out?

Signs That Your Teen is Struggling with Mental Health

"I thought that somebody has got to know the solution, somebody has got to know what I'm going through or how to deal with this, and then after so many times of not coming up with an answer the first

time, because I don't have patience, I just want things
to be over with. I want them to happen in a day." –
Sixteen-year-old

I'll start by debunking the myth that all depressed teens exhibit signs of struggling. If you look at Joy's case, there were no signs. She was doing well in school and was helpful at home and at church. She was not sleeping all day and talking back to authority. She was the picture of a perfect teenager. So, it's easy to see why her depression slipped through unnoticed yet quietly killing this young girl. And that's why we'll talk about what you can do as a parent to help your teen overcome depression–because your teen might not show any signs, but they could be dying inside.

But in most cases, teens will show signs that all is not well, and if this happens, you need to act on these signals. Examples include:

- **A lack of self-care:** With adults, you often tell that someone is going through a hard time when they somehow stop caring about their appearance. Their hair looks messed up. Oral hygiene is a forgotten aspect, and they seem lost in this poor state of hygiene. The same goes for when teens struggle mentally. You soon start noticing that they have let themselves go. A teen who would dress to the nines to do a TikTok video now seems disinterested in their appearance and almost wears pajamas to school, even when it's not Halloween.

- **Frequent mood swings:** One minute, your teen is happy and looks like they are on top of the world. And the next? They are throwing a tantrum because of a trivial event. So, you felt like you were on edge, unsure of what you will experience next. You never know what to expect from them, and it concerns you.

- **A change in eating habits:** Food consumption is a crucial indicator of your child's mental health. Occasionally skipping a meal or binging on snacks is normal–we all understand how hormones work and why your kid may want to change how they eat. But uncontrollable eating or excessive weight loss is a sign that your kid is not doing okay.

- **Difficulties in school:** Grades are not constant, so you can expect your kid to perform better or worse than they occasionally do. But what if your kid is on a consistent decline and does not seem to get better? Now would be the time to have your child assessed for dyslexia and other learning difficulties. But if these don't pan out, you may deal with a mental disorder.

- **A lack of interest in hobbies:** Your kid could do well in school, eat enough, and may seem to have a grasp on their emotions. But are they interacting with other kids? How invested are they in their hobbies? A key sign of depression is a lack of interest in things we often find exciting. Your kid could no longer feel the need to play with dolls or play dress-up. But a sudden loss of interest in social media, games, hangouts, outdoor and indoor activities without an alternative replacement is a warning sign. Growing out of hobbies is normal, but doing so without seeking another source of joy is a red flag.

- **A lack of energy:** Does your teen suddenly seem tired on all occasions? They seem too worn out to go out, seem to be moving at a snail's pace, and are almost always complaining about a lack of energy. You can even see it in how often they nap and how much they fuss about engaging in any hardcore activity – they just want to sit or sleep.

- **A change in sleeping patterns:** Like with food, sleep habits can change in two ways–your teen could sleep too much or too little. Ideally, your kid should nod off for about eight to ten hours each night. But if they are constantly sleeping much more or much less, trouble is a -calling.

- **Isolation:** We talked about teens needing their space in chapter six. It's healthy for them and you–there's no need to be in each other's spaces all the time. However, there's a difference between taking time off and isolating yourself from others. Most depressed teens isolate themselves because they feel misunderstood by their loved ones–they choose to hide away and be alone with their thoughts.

- **Drug abuse:** Some teens try to escape their thoughts by self-medicating. And what do they use? The usual alcohol, marijuana, pills, and other drugs push them deeper into the funk. Escapism is typical when dealing with depression, so if you notice your child using drugs, don't assume they are doing it to be cool. Instead, they might run away from their terrifying thoughts.

Again, I don't want to generalize and say that all teens will show such signs. Some will go about their days looking normal, yet they face the biggest hurdles in their lives. Others will be open about it and seek help. But often, teens will hide away and seek refuge in unsafe ways. So, if you notice any of these signs, you'll need to step in before your teen seeks an alternative coping method.

Does that mean your teen is depressed? Not at all–your kid could just be dealing with the usual moodiness that comes with adolescence. Or they could battle other mental disorders like anxiety and ADHD. So, don't assume that your kid is depressed just because they show some or all these signs. Leave the diagnosis to the experts.

Just to show you how easy it is to misdiagnose a mental health disorder, let's look at how depression differs from sadness.

Sadness vs. Depression: Why Knowing the Difference Could Save Your Teen

*"[Depression can be] addicting, conditioning, because if you're depressed for a long time, you might feel happy one day, but then it's like you go back to being depressed again. It feels like something's wrong if you're not having that sort of feeling." –***Fifteen-year-old**

We've all been sad, a natural reaction to things not going our way. Maybe it was after breaking up with a romantic partner, losing a job we loved, moving to a new town, losing a pet, having our computers crash on us, etc. We have all been there. And sometimes, it can last for weeks, casting us into a state of low energy, moodiness, and even lack of interest in hobbies. It sounds a bit like depression, does it not? So, how can you ensure you are not confusing sadness for depression or depression for sadness? Here are some pointers:

- **Emotional state vs. mental illness:** Can you tell which is which? I'll help you–sadness is a reaction to a negative event. So, while you might be sad, you might still find some joy in things you love. But with depression, you are in a state of persistent sadness coupled with a negative change in physical and psychological wellbeing.

- **Temporary vs. persistent:** Sadness passes away with time, so one day, you wake up, and you feel okay. Your teen might, for example, have lost a pet. For a few weeks, they may look sad and act out of habit, then one day, they start slowly acting like themselves. But a depressed teen will remain in that state for much longer and cannot seem to snap out of it.

- **Specificity vs. generality:** A teen can point out why they feel sad, e.g., they failed their term paper. Depression is not so easy to single out. All they know is that they feel sad and lethargic. Sometimes, a teen will point out a cause, but that cause is often a trigger rather than the sole reason.

Sadness affects a teen's mood for a day, week, or a month. But depression takes over their life, cutting across all aspects, including their psychology, physical wellness, and mental state. It changes their life and, if left untreated, can derail a teen from their true purpose, or worse.

So, is your teen depressed? Unlike sadness, which is subjective, depression requires a test. Here's the difference. I can say I am sad, and that would be it–nobody can come and tell me I am not sad or that I imagine it. Depression is much more involving. I can't just say I am depressed. Instead, I must go through a series of tests before a professional can confirm my fears. So, before assuming that your teen is **depressed**, please get them checked out by a health professional.

Is Your Teen Suicidal?

*"There's a little fog, this chain-mail wall where I can see out, and I can see what's going on, but I can't affect it." –**Eighteen-year-old***

Have you ever heard of the ***Blue Whale challenge***? It was a game administered to teens, which involved completing tasks to get to the next level. The tasks would start slow, like 'watch a horror movie' before progressing to more intense tasks like 'cut yourself.' The final stage required the teen to commit suicide. While some reports of the teen deaths remain unconfirmed, investigative studies have proven that the game was played far and wide and resulted in the deaths of tens of kids. Unfortunately, the Blue Whale Challenge is one of the many gimmicks on social media to encourage suicide among teenagers.

Sadly, not all depressed teens will exhibit suicide warning signs. But can you tell if your child is falling prey to such challenges? Each time I think about suicidal teens, I remember Joy and how she could have jumped off the top floor of a city building, showing no signs that she was not okay. But here is the thing–she asked for help. By asking her younger sister how she would feel about her death, she was grasping at a straw -anything to ground her and let her know that people still cared about her. Is your child crying out to you? Here are some telling signs:

- Your teen often jokes or talks about committing suicide. It can be in passing, or they can be vivid about it,
- Your teen vocalizes the desire to die, muttering things like "I would be better off dead."
- Your teen seems to have fantasies about dying and asks things like, "how many people do you think would attend my funeral?",
- Your teen writes, sings, or even narrates stories about death and suicide,
- Your teen is giving away things they love, almost as if they are preparing to leave this world,
- Your teen is suddenly engaging in dangerous activities and seems to push the limits, e.g., driving at high speeds or hiking at dangerous spots,
- Your teen is intent on saying goodbye to their loved ones, and it almost feels like a last farewell, and
- Your teen is actively searching for ways to kill themselves. Maybe they have stashed pills or weapons in their room.

Do you resonate with any such signs? Then, do not waste time; instead, call the national suicide hotline **NOW**. Time is of the essence, and each second counts.

What Causes Depression in Teens?

"Sometimes, I just get in these moods. I don't know what it is, but I just don't want to deal with anything, and then the slightest little thing, I can either start crying or yelling. I call them my 'freakouts.'" – **Seventeen-year-old**

When my son was going through a funk, I kept wondering what had gotten into him. Was it something I had said? Was I failing as a parent? I could not help but blame myself as I watched him walk through the house, almost zombie-like, unfeeling, numb, and shutting out the world. While he was not depressed, he had some depressive states, which were terrible. And as the therapist explained to me, there isn't anything such as one thing that pushes people into depression. Depression is a culmination of factors, and the more of these that one has, or the more intense they are, the worse the depression. So, what could bother your teen?

- **Genes:** Did you know that your genetic makeup can push you closer to depression? Studies show that teens from families where one or more members have suffered depression are at more risk than those who have not. So, if you or anyone else in your family has a history of depression, know that it could trickle down to your teen.

- **Bullying:** Has your child been verbally, physically, or psychologically attacked in the past? Maybe they had another child push them around in school, which took a toll on their self-esteem. Or your teen has suffered TDV (refer to chapter seven) and is now navigating how it made them feel. If your child has been when they felt hopeless or helpless, they are likely to feel depressed in their teen years. Oh, and you might not even be aware that it happened.

- **Other mental disorders:** Mental health problems are linked to each other. For example, a teen who suffers anxiety can feel depressed when the anxiety gets out of hand. The same goes for eating disorders, learning disorders, ADHD, self-injury, etc. Any condition that makes your teen feel helpless and alone will probably push them to the brink of depression.

- **Trauma:** Many people suffer from depression after experiencing a traumatic experience. It could be the loss of a loved one, a terrorist attack, an accident, an abusive childhood, and more. Has your teen had a rough time in recent or past years? That could contribute to their depressive mood. It only gets worse if they don't deal with it healthily.

- **Lack of support:** Are you supporting your child enough? Here's an example. Suppose your daughter has recently discovered that she prefers dating women and has a hard time at school. Are you giving her the support she needs? A teen experiencing hostility from their loved ones or a general lack of support can feel helpless and alone, making them feel depressed.

- **FOMO (The fear of missing out):** Can we talk about depression in Gen Zs without covering the influence of social media? Here's what the typical teen schedule looks like–wake up and check social media. Who did what last night and with who? Where is the party tonight? Who broke up, and who's hooking up with the cool kids? Then shower, and on the way to school, monitor the updates. Push through the classes, engage in your extracurricular activities, get home, do your homework, and all the while checking social media. So, a teen can feel like they are missing out on life by seeing just how much fun other kids are having. A is at a party, X is out shopping, Y just got a new phone, and the list continues. It's one thing after the other, and your teen may feel like they suck in life because they don't have so much going on, which impacts their life. Their self-esteem suffers, and they feel excluded, paving the way for hopelessness.

Have you heard of the unfortunate depression cycle? Here's how it works. The above causes are just a few that could cause your teen's depressive state. Let's assume that your teen feels depressed because of their poor grades. So, they sleep more and can't eat well, so they hardly have the energy to study. Then, when they sit for the next exam, they do even worse, which fuels the depression. Each time they fail, they get more depressed, making it harder to study, and sooner than they know it, they are in a cycle and cannot seem to find a way out. Can you see why getting out of such a funk can be problematic?

What You Can Do to Help Your Teen Overcome Depression

"I miss the little girl I was at times. I remember running in the streets barefooted in the summertime with all the neighborhood kids playing games every day...those are probably my happiest times, out having fun and being a kid. I grew up too quickly and missed that whole childhood thing, and I want to go back."

When our kids are younger, we are their protectors–we protect them from the clowns at birthday parties, kiss their scraped knees as we apply band-aids on them, and scare the ghosts under their beds. We stand by at the parks and ensure nobody touches or harms them and are always on standby, ready to pounce on anyone who dares to get too comfortable with them. We know how to fight these fights because we are wrestling with something we can see, touch, and feel. But how do we protect our kids from something we cannot see? - Something that destroys them from within? A disease that ravages them, robbing them of their light and casting them into the darkness? How do we reach in and pull them out, hoping that they are not too far gone by the time they wrap their hands around us?

- **Don't sit and wait:** Depression does not go away on its own. I know how tempting it can be to sit, hope, and pray that this phase will go away just like their terrible twos, but it won't. It's much deeper than a few tantrums in the store, so you must act as soon as you notice the symptoms. But how?

- **Talk to your teen:** Do you remember our communication tactics in chapter five? Now is the time to put them into practice. Ask your child what they are going through and **listen** to them as they walk you through their feelings. Don't probe too much, despite the urge to know as much as you can. Instead, create an environment where they can talk at their preferred pace, knowing they are heard. And let them know you are there to walk with them on the journey. Do not talk them out of depression. Even saying things like "You'll be fine" is not okay. Just acknowledge what they are feeling. If you are having trouble finding an appropriate answer, go through chapter five on communication blocks and avoid anything that falls under that umbrella.

- **Seek help:** If your teen does not want to open up to you, refer them to a trusted person. It could be a therapist, a school counselor, a GP, or anyone your teen is comfortable with. Sometimes, that's the best you can do as a parent.

- **Reduce their isolation time:** Depressed teens want to hideaway. While this helps them process their feelings, it pushes them further into the darkness. Allow them space but still, encourage them to interact with other people. Talk to them face to face, limit their time on social media, get them to join a club, get them to volunteer, etc. Anything that gets them out of the house and among other people is a welcome idea.

- **Get your teen to exercise:** Here's another cycle you need to break. Depression makes your teen feel lethargic, and they are less physically active. Unfortunately, mental and physical health are intertwined. So, if your kid is not active physically, their mental health suffers. When their mental health suffers, they shun physical activity even more. See the pattern? Combat this by getting your teen to exercise at least an hour every day. It should be something they enjoy, like riding a bike or swimming or even lifting weights if they are into that sort of thing. Couple the exercise with healthy meals and encourage your teen to sleep at least eight hours a day. It helps if you also engage in these activities to keep them company and motivate them to keep going.

- **Ask for help:** For a long time, talking about depression was taboo. People would hide what their loved ones were going through because of stigma of mental illnesses. But it only made the situation worse and prompted people to resort to negative escapism. Don't allow your child to follow that route. If your teen is not doing well, involve a professional who can diagnose if your child **is depressed** or suffering from another mental disorder. Allow your teen to choose the preferred path as you check out the different options. If a therapist does not connect with your child, find another who will. Also, seek second opinions when discussing any treatment options. While antidepressants work, they are often more effective when used with other treatment plans. And sometimes, teens don't need medication at all. So, unless your teen is at risk of harming themselves, take time to weigh the options and choose one that your teen wants. *Please note that antidepressants also come with an added risk of suicide, even in the first few months.*

- **Walk the talk:** Once you, your teen, and the professional have agreed on the best course of treatment, ensure you stay involved. Figure out how your teen is responding to the treatment, be understanding when they are having a hard time, and allow them to go through the motions.

• **Practice self-care:** As your teen goes through this tough time, it's easy to forget to care for yourself. But remember that you cannot pour from an empty cup. So, eat well, sleep enough, get help, talk to someone, stay active, and ensure that you are performing optimally. Only then can you be there for your child. Also, don't forget to look into the well-being of the other kids -are they okay? Are they feeling neglected?

Depression does not disappear instantly once your teen is in therapy or on treatment. They won't be back to feeling like themselves in a day or week, or month. Sometimes, it takes months for you to see a glimmer of hope in your teen's eyes. So, you need to be patient and trust the process. You might also need to start therapy to be better poised to be there for your child.

Is Untreated Depression That Bad?

I've come across people who think that depression goes away on its own. "Drink water, sleep enough, eat fruits and veggies, and you will be fine." That seems to be a universal cure for depression. But what people don't know is that while these activities are helpful, they account for a portion of the treatment. Depressed teens still need therapy, and some need to be on drugs. And oh, while drinking water and getting sleep might seem like a no-brainer, depressed teens might find that to be an uphill task. They can't bring themselves to do it–they don't want to, and they don't have the energy to do it. So even these simple tasks might not be options.

What happens to teens who don't get the help they need?

- They feel unloved and unwanted and choose to remain withdrawn from their peers and families,
- They cannot find the energy to keep up with sports or physical activity. So, exercising and being part of the team seems but a dream,
- The lack of interest, coupled with reduced concentration, makes it hard for them to do well in school. Their grades drop, and some even opt to stay out of school for good,
- They cannot relate with others because they do not feel like they deserve to be privy to social interactions. So,

they pull away, isolating themselves, which makes them even more depressed,

- They try to feel something by doing drugs or drinking alcohol, hoping that these substances will give them what it takes to sleep better, feel better, and be jovial. But unfortunately, the drugs only worsen their symptoms,

- They might engage in risky behaviors just to feel something other than nothing. They get involved in accidents, dating the wrong people, having unsafe sex, or even selling drugs. If you look at the population of teens engaging in the sex trade or drug peddling, the numbers are pretty high–especially in big cities. And you find that some of these teens willingly left their homes, dropped out of school, and were on the streets. Over time, they get wrapped up in messy schemes with adults who take advantage of them and sell them to the highest bidders. Of course, this changes a teen's life for the worse,

- Some teens resort to harming themselves. They cut their skin, hit themselves, pull out their hair, pick at their skin, anything to escape the nothingness within themselves. And this self-injury can get to where it endangers the teen,

- They harm others. Their anger or lack of love can propel a depressed teen to hurt others. They act out and can be verbally or physically abusive towards others–their way of expressing the pain inside. Unfortunately, this only alienates them from others, contributing to worse depression.

We've also covered how depression can drive a teen to suicidal thoughts and attempts. That's why we cannot ignore the signs.

What Happens When Parents Miss the Signs? The Blame Game.

*"It's not whether you win or lose. It's how you place the blame." –***Oscar Wilde**

I've talked about what can happen to a depressed teen– acting out, ending up on the streets, violence, etc. But what happens to parents who miss or ignore the signs until the depression gets to such a point? I'll start with a story. A couple I know has a lovely young teen girl. For as long as I have known her, she's been scoring As -not A-minus, but straight As. Then, along the road, her grades started dropping. One of her parents (A) voiced concern about it, imploring the other that it was time to act. But the other parent (B) felt like they were rushing it, and a drop in grades was normal. You can see that each parent thought they were doing what was right. One wanted to be proactive, and the other wanted to give the teen space.

As they waited, the grades dropped even further. Again, parent A wanted to step in, but parent B wanted to wait. Before they knew it, they had no option but to get involved. The reason?–their daughter was abusing drugs. So, they started the rehabilitation journey. Because the substance abuse was quite heavy, the teen had to be an inpatient. Months went by, with the teen popping in and out of rehab. Her senior year went by like that. A girl who was poised to be joining an Ivy League school was now home, ravaged by the effects of drugs. Her grades had dropped to Cs and Ds, and she was far behind her peers. But that was not the only effect–her parents were now constantly fighting. Parent A blamed parent B for waiting so long that their daughter had slipped through the cracks. And parent B felt their actions were justifiable because none of them could have seen this coming.

That's a marriage on the line. Often, we think about what happens to the teen, but the caregivers also get affected. Is there anything you can do when you miss the signs and start the blame game?

- **Own your part:** I know this is hard. But before you defend yourself, think of what you could have done to contribute to the sudden turn of events. For example, parent B could acknowledge that they could have been more involved at the onset. And parent A can own any part they played in it.

- **Apologize:** Try to look at the situation from your partner's point of view. Can you see why they might think you are to blame? What apologies do you think parents A and B can offer each other? Apologizing implies sincerity and creates room for conversation. Once you get the apologies out of the way, then you can start thinking of ways to help your teen. But if you are all stuck in your feelings, there's no way you can work together.

- **Question Your Thoughts:** Parent B might think they care more about their child than parent A. And parent A might also feel the same thing. Ask yourself if your thoughts are justifiable. Are you coming from a negative space? It's human nature to go to the worst likely scenario, especially when you feel like someone has let you down. But can you rationalize your thinking?

- **Let go of the need to be right:** The worst has happened. You've owned your part in it and apologized. You don't always have to be right. Sure, you thought your actions were in your child's best interests. But, likely, your partner thought so too. You might have approached the situation differently, but the goal was the same. So, stop chasing the need to be right and accept that your partner's experience is not the same as yours.

- **Forgive yourself:** You're likely to take on the blame for what's happened and beat yourself up about it. It's good that you are aware of your part in it. But wallowing in it won't let you be there for your child. So, take the steps necessary to forgive yourself – assess the situation, think of what you could have done differently, then let it go. It was a lesson, not a life sentence. And the more you dwell on it, the harder it can be to be there for your child.

- **Seek help:** With the blame game rearing its ugly head, you might want to bring in a neutral third party. A therapist would be a good idea at this point. You can both voice your concerns, keeping in mind that you have a teen to protect. That way, you can save your parental relationship (and romantic one where applicable) while saving your teen. Also, if the blame game takes a violent turn, seek safety. Don't wait to see what happens next.

Parenting guilt is normal, and situations like this can make it even worse. But no parent is perfect–nobody sees and reacts to all the signs. We all make mistakes. But the only way we become better parents is if we acknowledge human is to err. Then we can seek the help we need to be there for our children.

So, what happens if the *signs of depression* turn out to be warning signs that your child is battling anxiety? Find out in the next chapter.

***

Chapter Ten

The Anxious Teenager: Is Your Teen A Ball Of Nerves?

Social phobia or social anxiety: *an intense fear of social settings for fear of judgment and embarrassment. It also includes FOMO (the fear of missing out).*

W hen I think back to it, I admit it was easy to miss the signs because I missed them all. What am I talking about? A few years ago, my niece came to stay with us. She was seventeen, quite shy, and I thought the usual adolescence played its part. So, I knew little about it when she spent all day indoors. After all, she slept a decent number of hours, seemed to have control over how much time she spent on her phone, ate enough, exercised now and then, and was overall a level-headed teen. She helped around the house, cracked us up sometimes, and was very agreeable. But she hardly ever left the house, save for basking in the yard and taking a dip in the pool. Never past the gate, never at the neighbor's, never over twenty feet from the front door. Always inside the walls, almost as if she was afraid of what was behind those walls. And she was -only that I did not know. My niece was battling with anxiety, and I would never have known until her mother let me in on it, months after she had joined college.

"But how?" I asked, perplexed. "What made her anxious?"

"She felt judged," my sister offered, almost as if that would have answered the questions rushing through my mind. *Judged by who? By what? And why?*

Anxious. Just like depression, anxiety slowly eats away at the victim. So, your teen may look calm on the surface, but underneath that exterior is a teen struggling with sweaty palms, a racing heart, bewildered eyes, and shortness of breath.

Telling Signs that Your Teen's Anxiety is Problematic

Generalized anxiety disorder: Persistent worry about life situations, e.g., school, safety, health, the future.

I remember when my uncle came back from serving in the military. He was open about his flashbacks and the cold sweats he suffered in the night, dealing with one nightmare after the other. Despite being back at home, he lived in fear. PTSD, he called it. Post-traumatic stress disorder is now openly discussed, but it was hush-hush back then. My uncle chose not to live in silence and suffer alone. He decided to get help. And it was understandable–he had seen things, lost loved ones, and singling out the cause of his constant fear was somewhat easy.

But anxiety is not always that apparent. We don't always know the causes, and to make it worse, we might not even know what signs we should look for. Take me as an example. I spent months with an anxious teenager and thought she was just a shy introvert. I nurtured that anxiety without even knowing I was playing a part.

Can you tell that your teen is suffering from anxiety? Well, these signs can help you zero in on what might trouble your teen:

Physically

Do you want to know an interesting part about mental struggles? They also exhibit physically. So, while anxiety will not show up in lab tests and CAT scans, it will show as your teen is:

- Refusing to eat in public places or use public washrooms,
- Sweating profusely or shaking when they are in public settings,
- Looking tense, distracted, or restless when out in public,
- Complaining of aches and pains that don't seem to have a cause,
- Often feeling unwell and experiencing gastrointestinal issues,
- Changing their eating habits with the snap of a finger, and
- Experiencing insomnia.

The general takeaway is that your teen outwardly shows discomfort in situations where other people would be comfortable. And it does not happen once. It keeps happening. For example, my niece would come up with reasons not to leave the house. And when we finally were out, she would appear uneasy, walking on the far end, not making eye contact, choosing tables that were far from other people, preferring to pack the food and go rather than sit at the food court–the signs were always there.

Emotionally

Of course, it's easy to get worked up when you're facing a condition that only you can feel. So, an anxious teen:

- Often suffers panic or anxiety attacks.
- Is not comfortable making mistakes–they fear being judged and cannot help but try to avoid attracting more attention.
- Can suffer emotional outbursts regularly–crying, showing irritability, getting angry for no reason. While teens are often emotional, so an anxious teen takes it to the next level. Plus, they are not open to criticism, even the constructive kind.
- Does not seem confident in their abilities. Such a kid will be great at something, but ask them to show the world, and they shrink away.

- Seems lost in concerns about the future - always wondering what will happen next and not living in the moment.

Some teens will also experience obsessive thoughts or worries about negative events. Such thoughts will not show on the surface. Still, as we covered earlier, they will instead present as physical signs or changes in their emotional patterns. But remember that teens can show some of these changes without suffering from an anxiety disorder. So, it often gets tricky when drawing the line between normal teenage reactions and anxiety. But an anxiety attack would be a clear sign that anxiety is to blame for the sudden changes.

Behaviorally

My niece was relatively quiet and often kept to herself, which we all thought was a shy individual. But she had not always been like this–I had raised her for a few years when she was younger, and I'd known her to be more interactive. So, I blamed the teenage hormones. But it turns out that her behavior change was another sign that anxiety was crippling her life. So, how does it show in teens' behaviors?

- **Avoidance of social interactions:** Be it speaking in class or attending a party, an anxious teen will do what it takes to avoid such a setting. Sometimes, a kid prefers a quiet space, but the kid faces anxiety at others.

- **Avoiding schoolwork:** It's one thing for a kid to shun parties, but what of group work and team activities? Anxiety could be blamed if a teen remains silent or does not seem interested in these activities.

- **Refusal to interact with others:** Most teens jump at the chance to meet other people and will often interact with strangers at the slightest opportunity. But an anxious teen prefers not to do so and can be silent or aggressive when meeting new people.

- **A tad of separation anxiety:** Anxious teens prefer familiar environments and can get emotional or irritable when away from their homes and loved ones.

- **An increase in emotional outbursts:** A kid who would push back when asked to do chores now explodes when asked to do something outside their comfort zone.

- **An incline into compulsive behaviors:** Anxious teens may seem obsessed with washing their hands, keeping their rooms clean, arranging stuff, etc. It's their way of having control over the situation. If this behavior crops up, pay more attention.

Please keep in mind that anxiety disorders are different and will thus exhibit in different ways. Your teen could suffer from one or more of these disorders, and their behavior may match one or more of the signs we have covered above. So, once you realize your teen is struggling, narrow it down to the specific anxiety they are experiencing.

Causes and Dangers of Anxiety in Teenagers

Specific Phobias: An intense fear about a situation or object, e.g., speaking in public, dogs, heights, spiders. Results in avoidance.

"I had just realized that I had not done well on my first case study and was walking to the store. The news had hit me hard, and I needed to buy a snack before heading home. I was standing in line, and then I felt it — the fast heartbeat, the shortness of breath, the unexplainable fear, a tinge of dizziness, and a dry mouth. I was scared, unsure of what was happening to me, and unable to move. I bought my snack and headed home, feeling my heart beating like crazy. Then I got home and paced around, and I could still feel my heart beating. So, I went to the hospital, and they diagnosed me with an anxiety attack–I did not have a heart attack. That only confused me even further–what was an anxiety attack?"

That was my niece explaining what had happened to her after receiving her results on her first term paper. She was eighteen, having just joined college and having her first anxiety attack. While she admitted to having suffered anxiety for as long as she could remember, that was the first time it had affected her physically. And that was the first time she had opened up to her mom about what had been happening. It was the first of many steps on her road to living with anxiety. I could not help but wonder what would have happened to her had she suffered the anxiety attack while driving on a highway, crossing the street, or doing anything that required her full attention. I could not understand what was causing her anxiety. Are you in the same boat, wondering what could trigger this unease in your kid?

Studies show that anxiety in teens could stem from:

- **Genes:** Like with depression, anxiety also comes down to family history. So, if you or someone in your family has suffered anxiety, it's likely to affect your kid.

Sometimes, it's also in the way you bring up your child. Say, for example, that you are an anxious parent, constantly worrying about something–your child can pick this up and start exhibiting similar patterns. So, with the whole nature vs. nurture question, both may win in this case.

- **The brain function:** Everyone boasts a different brain structure, particularly the amygdala, which controls our fight-or-flight responses. Teens with anxiety often have a hypersensitive amygdala, which explains why they may react more sharply to otherwise mundane situations.

- **Childhood traumas:** Kids who go through tough times will probably suffer anxiety and other mental conditions as adults. Often, the signs show in early adulthood, though they can creep up even in adolescence. Examples include childhood abuse, separation from parents, losing a loved one, bullying, etc.

- **Unrealistic expectations:** Without getting into FOMO, let's consider what the average teen must do to excel. Doing well in school and getting A's on all subjects is no longer enough. Instead, they must also be good at after-school activities, volunteer, help at home, maintain an active social life, etc. But, of course, excelling in all these things means they must sacrifice their alone time, depriving them of rest and sleep. And you can imagine that even when they eventually nod off, they are still wondering how they can have the edge over the competition.

But unrealistic expectations are not all about schoolwork. Sometimes, it's in the way parents handle their kids' emotions. Can you remember the communication blocks we talked about in chapter five? It's become quite normal for parents to step in and process their children's emotions on their behalf. For example, rather than letting your kid process the death of a pet or anything that makes them sad, you may think it's okay to step in and cheer them up. Sure, that helps them move through the grieving quicker. But it also hinders your child from learning that it's normal to experience negative emotions like sadness, guilt, anger, frustration, etc. When they finally face a situation where they have no choice but to face these emotions, they feel anxious because they do not know how to do so.

Let's get a bit into the 'yes' parenting technique I talked about in chapter six and why this can make your teen anxious. Some parents believe in reinforcing their kids' beliefs in themselves by vocalizing it often. *You are the most creative student in your class. You are the most gifted artist in your grade.* The list goes on and on - do you know what this communicates?–that your child must live up to this pedestal. After all, if you are the most creative student in your class, why would you not come up with the best project? It causes your teen to feel anxious whenever they have to do anything that might jeopardize this perfection their parents have dreamed up.

- **Social pressure:** Now, let's get a bit into FOMO. Gen Zs live in a world filled with social pressures, some positive and others negative. For example, your kid's friends are all getting into good schools and have extraordinary dating lives. As a result, your teen may feel the need to keep up and feel anxious about not performing at their peers' levels. It's even worse for them because these successes play out right in front of them–on their social platforms, triggering them each time they log onto such apps.

- **Substance abuse:** Teens experiencing anxiety may seek refuge in drugs, worsening their anxiety. Sure, the drugs may help them escape reality for a while. But when the effects wear off, the anxiety is even worse because it comes in two-fold. One in how long it takes the teen to get their hands on drugs, and two in the anxiety they were experiencing before taking the drugs. This compounding throws the teen into a voracious cycle that keeps eating into their peace of mind.

- **Depression:** Did you know that anxiety and depression are related? For example, it's easy to confuse anxiety for depression. You may notice that your kid stays indoors for long hours and has a limited social life, and you may think they are depressed. While, in truth, they are suffering from social anxiety. Unfortunately, anxiety could pave the way for depression. For example, a teen who continuously avoids doing things and meeting people may become so isolated that they end up depressed. In the same way, a depressed teen could feel so anxious about being around others for fear of being misunderstood. Sometimes, a teen can suffer from both or could be experiencing one of these disorders, which could pave the way for the other if left untreated.

Is anxiety such a big deal? Should you be worried about your kid living in fear? Why, yes! Studies show that anxious teens often doubt their abilities so much that it eventually erodes their confidence and self-esteem. Eventually, they shun the outside world, choosing to be recluses, and can fall into depression. So, if you've noticed that your teen has exhibited the above signs, you should not take them lightly.

Are You Playing a Role in Your Teenager's Anxiety?

Panic disorder: An overwhelming feeling of fear in a situation that would otherwise feel normal to most people. Related to agoraphobia, where people avoid places where panic attacks can occur.

When my niece sought help for her anxiety, the therapist suggested attending some sessions with my sister. Of course, my sister was appalled at the thought. *"Does the therapist want to blame me for what my child is going through? What could I have possibly done to make my child anxious?"* It was one question after the other as she geared up for her first session. Finally, with her defenses ready, she walked into that office, prepared to defend her actions as a parent. And a few weeks later, she came over for a cup of tea, this time calmer, having picked up a few integral points. As she walked me through what she had learned, I got to see just how easily well-meaning parents could trigger anxiety in their kids. Unknowingly, we had *enabled* my niece's anxiety, not realizing that we were only making the situation worse.

So, how can parents contribute to anxiety in their kids?

- **Being too accommodating:** We have different parents –those that push their kids too hard, those that use just enough balance, and those that don't push at all. Now, let's talk about the complaisant parents. For example, your teen feels too eager to go to school, and you figure that homeschooling is the answer. Or they are too nervous about going camping, so you cancel the trip at the last minute. It's great that you want to be there for your kid. Still, you may be unwittingly communicating that it's okay to run away from discomfort–that if something feels too hard, your teen can run!

- **Not being accommodating at all:** So, we can agree that being too complaisant does not alleviate a teen's anxiety. It only helps them rest in their cocoon, knowing they never need to come out. But what if you were to push the kid into the outside world even if they were anxious? What if you forced them to go to school teary-eyed and scared? Or pack up and go camping despite their pleas? Well, your heart would be in the right place, but the delivery would worsen their anxiety. How about teaching them some coping mechanisms first?

- **Fighting their battles:** So, you see your kid anxious about talking to strangers. And because you want them to feel comfortable around people, you take it upon yourself to introduce them to new people. Good job!– Only that unless your teen takes the initiative, you are not helping them. You push them to depths they probably cannot swim in now. Allow them to move at their pace. If greeting one stranger a week is all they can do, then so be it. The added pressure will only worsen their anxiety.

- **Misinterpreting the anxiety:** I am guilty of this one. When my niece would stay in all day, I would tell people she was a shy introvert. *She enjoys being home and reading books all day.* That was my way of interpreting why she would rather stay indoors than attend a party, go shopping, or trail me on my trips. I've heard all sorts of misinterpretations over the years. *He's just lazy and does not want to leave the house. She's just looking for an excuse not to spend time with us. He just wants to skip school.* I don't blame the parents. After all, if you have never experienced anxiety, it's hard to

213

tell that it's what's crippling a teen. It's just easier to blame it on the teen. But here is the thing -nobody wants to live in fear. If a teen had the choice between being out there and being stuck in their head, they would prefer the first option. So, being a bit more understanding can help your teen fight this battle.

Oh, and there's also the assumption that anxiety always results from trauma. It's not always the case - sometimes, it's just genetics. So, skip asking *why* even when evidence points to biological factors. And instead, focus on helping your teen.

Is it Time to Call for Help?

Separation anxiety disorder: The fear of being away from a loved one or home.

We all feel anxious. For example, maybe we're moving to another city and do not know how we feel about it. Or we've started a new project and are unsure what the outcome will be. In most of these cases, the anxiety passes, and we feel better in no time. But anxiety in teens may not be so temporary. So, how do you know that your teen's anxiety is no longer manageable, and they might need help?

- They are abusing drugs,
- Their grades have suffered,
- They appear restless,
- Their eating or sleeping habits have changed for the worse,
- They no longer engage in their hobbies,
- They have isolated themselves,
- They seem to experience negative emotions, e.g., fear, sadness, anger, worry,
- They are showing signs of depression,
- They are engaging in destructive behaviors, e.g., cutting themselves, and
- They are talking about death or seem to harbor suicidal thoughts.

Have you noticed any of these signs in your child? Then it's time you sought help from a professional therapist. Remember that untreated anxiety could cause depression and vice versa, so the sooner you deal with it, the better.

But of course, your teen may not view therapy the way you do. They might even think of it as punishment and could shun the whole idea. So, how do you get your teen to go to therapy? You talk about it positively. Instead of saying, *"You need therapy because you stay home all day and do not interact with other kids,"* you could say, *"I have noticed that you spend a lot of time at home of late and are not interacting with your peers as much. Therapy is a safe space where you can talk about what may have caused these changes."* Also, add that what they share in therapy will remain confidential. So, if you've been causing your child anxiety, they'll know they can share this with the therapist with no backlash.

Equipping Your Teen with Coping Mechanisms

Obsessive-compulsive disorder: Exhibits in a series of compulsive thoughts or actions geared at quelling anxiety, e.g., clapping twice before sleeping to keep nightmares at bay.

Aha! We are now talking about how you can help your child navigate their anxiety. Is there anything you can do? Is there a way to help them manage their anxiety attacks even when alone? Well, it all starts with:

- **Communication:** We will always go back to chapter five: communication. If your teen does not feel comfortable talking to you about mundane topics, you can bet they won't speak to you about their anxiety. Open up communication so your child can tell you what makes them anxious. For example, if your son feels anxious about going to the store, find out why he feels this way. You can even brainstorm together about why they are worried about that situation. Then you can understand his anxiety and help him manage it better.

- **Acknowledgment:** Anxiety is not imagined. It's real, and it affects your teen. So, if your daughter comes home and does not want to do her exam because she's afraid she will fail, don't tell her not to worry. Or change the subject or any of the communication blocks we covered. Instead, acknowledge her anxiety and let her know you believe she can handle it. And that if she needs extra help, you will be there as needed.

- **Affirm:** We live in an age of self-affirmations. So, how about using this to help your kid? Start small. For example, they cannot cross the street because they are anxious. Start building their confidence by having them mutter. *I can do this. I have crossed the street before and can do it again.* Once they have practiced this self-talk for a while, you can ask them if they are ready to put it to the test. Another way of helping your teen is by teaching them to be self-compassionate. We are often hung up on helping others and sometimes take a backseat. So, if your teen feels off because of their anxiety, teach them to speak positively about themselves. *It's okay to feel anxious about crossing the street. That does not make me....* They can insert any negative feelings they may have about themselves at this juncture, e.g., that does not make me *a weirdo.*

Finally, encourage your teen to ask for help. For example, suppose your daughter feels anxious about going to the mall alone. You can ask her to request you to tag along. Sometimes, having someone by their side can help them take that first step into being more confident.

- **Praise:** We are not talking about being a 'yes' parent who claps at everything their child does. Instead, praise your child when they do something they wouldn't have done before because of anxiety. Say your child could not order something at a restaurant because they were crippled with anxiety. Now, let them know you see how far they have come each time they do. This praise acknowledges their baby steps and gives them the confidence to try even more things.

But all these tactics lean on the parental side. Is there anything your kid can do to manage their anxiety better? There sure is!

- **Understanding the signs of anxiety:** Anxiety often presents in different ways. It could be in a faster heartbeat, sweaty palms, etc. Have your child write any anxious moments and how they made them feel. Once they know the key signs, they can know when they will feel anxious and can start enforcing their coping strategies, e.g., maybe your teen has difficulty breathing when feeling anxious.

- **Understanding the triggers:** Does your teen know what makes their anxiety worse? The more they can narrow down on these, the easier it is to manage the anxiety. For example, I came across a teen who could not read any story about injustice without feeling triggered. And the more she felt triggered and scared, the more she read news about injustice, hurling her into a dark cycle. So, her therapist suggested she take time off social media until she gained better control over her social media usage.

- **Engaging in anxiety-reducing exercises:** Is there anything that makes your child feel less anxious? It could be journaling, dancing, painting, exercising, watching movies, cooking, etc. Encourage them to experiment with different activities to figure out what makes them feel calm. Then, when they feel the signs of anxiety, they can engage in the said activity as we described above.

- **Relaxing more:** Escapism often takes precedence when dealing with anxiety. But how about embracing the anxiety? Mindfulness has proven to be a great help when dealing with anxiety. Activities such as yoga and meditation allow your teen to feel the anxiety and release it, making them feel calmer in the long run. However, not everyone takes to these activities. So, if your teen does not feel better after meditating or doing yoga, allow them to find what works for them.

- **Exercising, sleeping, hydrating, and eating healthy foods:** A healthy body equals a healthy mind. Encourage your teen to take better care of themselves. Besides, studies show that active teens are at less risk of developing anxiety–getting that heart rate up through cardio can help your teen alleviate some of their symptoms.

- **Spending less time on social media:** Our kids are almost always on their phones, a form of escapism that can worsen their anxiety. Encourage your child to spend more time with their loved ones. This one-on-one interaction aids in grounding them and can reduce the feelings of isolation that come with FOMO. If talking does not work, you can try eating out, engaging in sports, or doing any other activity that gets them off that phone.

- **Cutting off caffeine:** More kids are getting hooked on caffeine at an early age. I would like to get into the effect of this stimulant on their brains, but I know it can make for quite a debate. However, we can agree that stimulants can worsen the symptoms of anxiety. So, as your kid works through their anxiety, encourage them to cut off coffee, sodas, and any other caffeinated goodies.

Even with all these measures in place, your kid may still feel anxious. Therefore, I encourage you to combine these anxiety alleviation strategies with therapy. The professional can then weigh the benefits of therapy, meds, or a combination to see what suits your child.

Oh, and just like with depression, anxiety does not go away. Sometimes, your teen may think they are over it, then one day, it rears its ugly head, ready to devour them. So, you will need to be patient as you walk them through this process. And remember to take care of yourself so you don't fall apart when trying to piece your kid's life together.

***

Chapter Eleven

How Do You Handle Emotional Whirlwinds In Teenagers?

"Bitterness is like cancer. It eats upon the host. But anger is like fire. It burns it all clean." — **Maya Angelou**

I can't count the number of times my teen and I would get into a fight that ended up in them leaving the room in a huff. Then, moments later, I would hear the door slam. And to make sure I had heard it, they would sometimes slam the door again, just for effect. I often considered unhinging that door and putting it away in storage. Then they would have nothing left to slam. But of course, I knew this would not work. A friend had tried this to keep her child 'in check.' A month later, she had fixed the door, realizing that her daughter still had other doors to slam -the fridge doors, car doors, doors in different rooms in the house, pretty much anything that could open and shut. So, I would stand or sit in the kitchen or living room, sometimes with tears welling up in my eyes, wondering how we had gotten here. Why could we not just get through some conversations without such harsh reactions? Was I approaching communication wrongly? Was I pushing too hard and causing this backlash? Sure, there are times I played a part in how my child reacted. Still, the cause of this apparent anger boiled down to other factors that I had not considered until I started exploring teen anger.

Why Teenagers Have Outbursts

"Anger is an acid that can do more harm to the vessel in which it is stored than to anything on which it is poured." — **Mark Twain**

Teen anger: I am sure almost every parent with a teenage child has experienced this. It comes out of nowhere, fast, and knocks you off your feet. Then, as if nothing happened, your teen emerges from their room, ready for round two, or acts as if they have no clue what happened. Why does this happen? Chapter four covered the teenage brain and why adolescents do not act like adults. They are still in that phase between childhood and adulthood, with their prefrontal cortex still developing. The result?–they experience wildly different emotions, which trigger their impulsiveness.

As they battle with this increased sensitivity, they are also more aware that they are no longer children. So, they do not appreciate being babied -they want to have a seat at the table and enjoy a say about what happens in their lives. That's why they push back when you try to impose your opinion on matters that they feel are their business. So, you suddenly begin arguing about who they should date, political interests, spiritual issues, and a hoard of other topics in which you initially had the final word.

But before you put your foot on the floor and say that your word is the law, consider what your teen is feeling. We have talked about walking in your teen's shoes. Now, let's picture being a teen and:

- **Being self-conscious:** Your teen wakes up one day, and they suddenly have hormonal and body changes. And we all know that these changes can go either way and can catapult your teen to feel embarrassed and vulnerable. Some teens feel less than when they see just how well others are taking to their new bodies. Oh, and if there's bullying involved, the self - consciousness only gets worse. So, imagine going through all this and feeling misunderstood. Wouldn't you also feel a tinge of anger?

- **Feeling frustrated:** Your teen is no longer a baby and does not want to be seen as a child. So, each time you don't **listen** to what they want and decide to impose what you want, you frustrate them. Add that they are highly emotional and impulsive, and you have a recipe for teen anger.

- **Feeling isolated:** Teen friendships change a lot -cliques form at this age. So, your kid might have been hanging out with a group of friends who are suddenly too cool for them now. Getting phased out of friendships can be hard on a teen. It's even worse with social media -some teens get to be so popular with their TikTok and Instagram numbers blowing up. Others get to be on the sidelines, watching their friends distancing themselves from the fray. And given how important it is to be visible in this digital age, this FOMO can get to them. *Why are they not blowing up?*

- **Feeling pressured:** Have you put too many expectations on your child? Studies show that Gen Zs are highly entrepreneurial and have a knack for academic excellence. So, on their own, they are go-getters who will put some pressure on themselves. Now add parental, teacher, and peer expectations. The weight of all this can be so much that they act out in anger.

- **Dealing with anxiety:** We talked about signs and causes of anxiety in the last chapter. A key sign of unmanaged anxiety is increased irritability. The slightest things seem to offend your teen, and you cannot fathom why this is the case. Anytime you ask them to do something, they respond aggressively, almost as if you have attacked them. But it's because they no longer feel safe and are in fight-or-flight mode.

So, you can see that while the anger may seem to come out of nowhere, there are many reasons your teen could lash out at you. And you can also see that you may contribute to it a great deal.

Is Your Teenager Acting Out?

"Most misunderstandings in the world could be avoided if people would simply take the time to ask, "What else could this mean?" — **Shannon L. Alder**

I remember breaking into a cold sweat that night as I called almost everyone I knew. It was about half-past seven o'clock, and I had just walked into the house. A few minutes of calling out my son's name without a response was all I needed to know that he was not home. We'd argued that evening–he wanted to attend a party with a few friends outside town, and I had refused to give in. *You never let me do anything!* That sentence kept ringing through my mind. His phone was off, his friends had not seen him, and all my neighbors did not know where he was. I was about to go to the police (never mind the 24-hour wait rule) when I got a call. My sister assured me that my son was okay and would spend the night with them. And as I thanked her and breathed a sigh of relief, I could not help but wonder if his anger was getting out of control. Was this normal?

I've had parents discuss the same thing–at what point do you know it's typical teen anger? Where do you draw the line? Is your child acting out or reacting to the circumstances?

Okay, so let's start with the fact that teen anger is normal. Teenagers get angry over small things and can stay that way for days and even weeks. Sometimes, it's justifiable, and sometimes, you just can't understand why they seem so angry. But they are because they are impulsive and emotional. Oh, and if you can recall chapter four, I stated that their conscience is still not well developed. So, they don't think about the consequences as much as we do. So, for example, when you are not happy about your work hours, you do not cuss at your boss. Instead, you go through the standard channels at work, negotiating a better option. But frustrate a teen, and what do they do?

- Slam doors
- Yell back
- Post angry captions on social media
- Run away
- Threaten to do something to themselves
- Rant about how you never let them do anything
- Talk about how bad you are as a parent
- Compare their lives to that of other teens or your parenting style to that of other parents

- Sulk, grouch, moan about what you have done or not done

The list goes on–you know how it goes, and you can even add what your teen has put you through. And sometimes, they express their anger with no filter, not thinking about how it affects you. But is this normal? Yes!

As your teen tries to be more **independent** and become their own person, you often lock heads. On the one hand, you want to exercise **control** over your child. But they want to be treated as adults and don't take well to hearing a 'no' from you or anyone else. So, the cycle begins, and they lose their temper at the slightest things. Remember the causes of teen anger we covered earlier–anytime these pain points come up. You will probably experience some anger from your teen.

The good news is that arguing is healthy, as it shows that your teen is now coming into their own. And if your teen wants to do this often, be happy that they are articulating their needs, albeit not always in the way you prefer. But at least there's some communication, and with some tips at hand, you can help your teen verbalize their frustration better.

The only problem comes in when their anger escalates to:

- Verbal abuse
- Physical abuse
- A blatant disregard for boundaries

If your teen has not crossed these lines, they are not acting out and are just going through the phases of prefrontal cortex development. Hold on–it won't last forever!

Signs That Your Teenager is Calling Out for Help

*"It is wise to direct your anger towards problems, not people; to focus your energies on answers, not excuses." — **William Arthur Ward***

Do you know why teenagers walk out on their parents or slam doors in their faces? They need to release that anger. So, they do what they think fits the moment. They scream, they yell, bang on tables, roll their eyes, stomp their feet, and do whatever it takes to release that frustration. But, of course, this only helps them in the short term. However, they still don't get the results they wanted–a resolution in the long term.

Screaming and yelling, while annoying, are normal. So, how do you know your teen is not handling their anger well?

- **They are verbally aggressive:** They have resorted to taunting others, using obscene language, publicly embarrassing others, sarcasm, being mean, and using their words to damage others. This behavior may be directed to you, siblings, peers, strangers, teachers, or anyone who encounters your teen.

- **They are physically aggressive:** Slamming doors and banging on tables is okay. But what happens when your teen puts a fist through the wall, threatens to beat up, or *actually* beats up someone in the heat of the moment?

- **They don't observe boundaries:** We talked about the need to observe boundaries with our teens–it's a great way to reduce that tension as they push for more independence during adolescence. So, what if your teen continuously ignores the boundaries? For example, you set a curfew for 8 pm, and they almost always come home after midnight. And even when you take away their privileges, they don't seem fazed. What happens then?

Teen anger that reaches into verbal and physical aggression or disrespect is problematic and requires more than patience from your side. One or two incidents are okay, and you can work through this. But if your teen is constantly getting into fights or threatening to do so, there's a problem. It's especially bad if you feel the need to avoid angering them because you are **afraid** of their reaction. Don't wait any longer–get professional help. The escalated anger could point to:

- **A mental health condition:** We have covered how anxiety and depression affect our children in the last two chapters. But these are not the only conditions that start showing in teen years. Your child could also exhibit signs of bipolar disorder, OCD, and a myriad of other conditions that require professional intervention.

- **Substance abuse:** Have you noticed any added secretiveness in your child? Are they hanging out with a new group of friends? Do you have any reason to believe that your child could do drugs? Unfortunately, substance abuse can heighten teen anger and make it much harder for you to manage your teen's frustration.

If you feel that your teen's anger has gone past normal and has gotten to where it could harm them or people close to them, consult a mental health professional. If you think they (or you) could be in danger, please contact the nearest hospital or police for immediate intervention.

Negativity in Teenagers: How to Snap Your Teenager Out of It

"Never respond to an angry person with a fiery comeback, even if he deserves it. Don't allow his anger to become your anger." — **Bohdi Sanders**

Have you ever met an angry teen? My son had his moments as an adolescent, and people who met him in one of his moods probably thought he was one. We would argue about something at home, and he would carry his anger with him. So, he'd be groaning in the backseat, facing away, probably dreaming of another world where he could get everything he wanted. Then he'd moan through whatever event I had dragged him to–sitting in the corner, scowling, and with his arms crossed. Sometimes, he would stare at his phone throughout the event–be it a wedding, conference, wake, family reunion, etc. He would be there, angry at me, angry at the world, just angry. Eventually, that anger would get to me, and I would be angry at him, angry at the world, plain angry. Was there another way to deal with this negativity? Sure!

- **Communication:** Chapter five of this book will remain a core contributor to the rest of the chapters. Why? Because when that door is open, your child can walk through it, knowing that they will be *heard* and will not be *judged*. When I finally started *listening* to my son, I realized he was remorseful when he acted out of anger. We would talk and get down to why he had acted that way. What was bothering him? Was there another way to deal with the underlying cause of anger? Sometimes, the issues were simple, and at others, we had to put our heads together to come up with a solution. But as long as we were talking *to each other*, he was happy. And if you want to have effective communication, remember to be calm even when your teen comes at you screeching. If you can't be calm, reschedule the conversation because going in hot-headed will only escalate the issue.

- **Encouraging a healthy lifestyle:** While high expectations, FOMO, hormones, and frustration are often the leading causes of teen anger, anger sometimes boils down to the lifestyle. Is your teen eating well?

How are they sleeping? Are they getting enough physical exercise? A child that leads a well-rounded lifestyle is less likely to feel cranky. Should I add you should lead by example? You can't be chugging two liters of soda and pointing out that your kid needs to drink more water–unless you want to frustrate them even more and heighten that anger.

- **Embracing the anger:** Sure, you don't like it when your teen acts out of anger. But they have a right to feel what they feel. Whether they are anxious, frustrated, isolated, do not know why they feel the way they do, it's their right. So, don't belittle what they are going through by asking them to *get over it* or *stop acting like a brat*. Instead, walk them through what is acceptable when they are angry. Do you remember the boundaries we covered in chapter six? Now might be the time to revisit them and include how you and your teen should act when angry.

- **Imparting anger management skills:** Do you remember the coping strategies we covered for teens battling anxiety? You can do the same thing for teens who seem to struggle with anger. Walk them through some activities to get a better grasp of their emotions. For example, they could listen to music, journal, talk to a trusted friend, or sleep. Anything that helps them deal with their anger healthily is a good idea.

- **Being consistent:** Part of helping your teen manage their emotions better is staying true to the set boundaries. You can't take away their privileges one time and the next; you give in to their demands. Doing this would only communicate that outbursts are acceptable in your household.

I followed through on these tips I gathered from my therapist and friends. So, does that mean that my son suddenly became an angel child that never got angry? No, getting angry is part of adolescence–you remember that whole prefrontal cortex thing, right? So, no matter how much you attend to your child, they will still get angry. The key is to help them learn how to cope with their anger and avoid crossing the line. My son still had his days, but he carried less anger with him as time went by and enjoyed happier than angry days. He was better for it, and so was I.

Are You Throwing Tantrums at Your Teen?

"Learn this from me. Holding anger is poison. It eats you from inside. We think that hating is a weapon that attacks the person who harmed us. But hatred is a

curved blade. And the harm we do, we do to ourselves." — **Mitch Albom**

You'd think that because I am writing this book, I was the parent that never erred when raising a teen. But that's not the case. While I did not unhinge my teen's door, I sometimes reacted to match his pace even when he slammed it. He would walk out of the room, and so would I. I would go, *"Oh, so you are walking out? Watch me do that too!"* Or be silent when he chose not to talk to me. He would sit on one side of the room, and I would be on the other side, flipping through a book or paper. *Two can play that game,* I would assure myself. But obviously, that did not work, and I had to use the coping mechanisms I covered earlier to help him through his fits. And help me too.

Why am I telling you this? Well, I know how tempting it can be to meet your teenager where they are–when they go low, you also want to go low and show them just how annoying their behavior is. But it does not make things better. It sets the ball rolling for more arguments.

So, how can you avoid throwing tantrums with your kid? Instead of making the argument about you, your feelings, and your bruised ego (I can relate to this one), I advise that you:

- **Don't escalate the situation:** Nobody likes to be on the losing side of an argument. It feels better to be the one who has the final word. So, when your teen has an outburst and says something cruel, you might have the perfect comeback for it. After all, we've been around long enough to know which remarks can cut deep. But think about this: will your response help or *hurt* the situation? Will your teen feel better about it? Will you? Cool down and avoid worsening the situation until you have something positive to contribute to the argument.

- **Control your emotions:** You cannot control how your teen feels or reacts–it's not up to you. It's not even up to them–they have this whole prefrontal cortex thing going. So, once you understand that their emotions and impulses are almost out of their control, you only have your emotions to consider. Are you doing the best you can to remain calm in the situation? Are there any anger management techniques you can employ when dealing with your angry teen? You can take a walk, meditate, do some yoga, breathe, call a therapist, anything that helps you stay in check. I would walk around the neighborhood and return when I felt I was in the right state of mind to address my son.

Parenting is more of a *monkey see; monkey do* scenario. So, staying calm communicates that it's possible to control one's emotions even when things don't go right. For example, if your teen sees you calmly walking away from a tense situation rather than shouting, or threatening them, they will learn by example. But if they see you kicking at doors and screaming at them, they will know that this is okay and start acting out. Be a role model in the behavior you want your child to emulate, and this will make the situation at home much better.

Enabling your teen to manage their anger is important. Right now, their actions may not have significant consequences. But fast forward to when they are eighteen and decide to act out–will the world be as accommodating as you are? Probably not, and that can derail them from succeeding later in life. So, don't wait until your kid learns the hard way. And I leave you with one last quote to sum up this topic:

"If you are patient in one moment of anger, you will escape a hundred days of sorrow." **–Chinese Proverb**

***

Chapter Twelve

Body Dysmorphia In Teenagers

Body dysmorphic disorder symptoms are becoming increasingly common in male teenagers. Nearly three percent of the Australian population reports body dysmorphic symptoms. Among Australian adolescent boys, twelve percent met the criteria for an eating disorder characterized by marked body image disturbances. Around twenty percent of German child/adolescent boys felt fat, fifteen percent were terrified of gaining weight, and twenty-five percent reported regularly feeling upset about weight or shape.

When Khloe Kardashian's unedited picture found its way to Instagram, the celebrity all but lost her mind. In the admittedly beautiful picture, there was no evidence of photo-shopping. Instead, it was a lovely picture, showing the thirty-six-year-old mother of one enjoying a sunbath by the beach–no-frills, nothing added, just sheer simplicity. And the result? Well, people loved it! They could not get enough of how relatable the picture was, with the lighting showing a dimple here, maybe a crease there, and the overall depiction of a healthy female body. But Khloe? She could not rest until the picture was off her page and the internet–completely scrubbed off. It did not align with the filtered and photo-shopped images scattered over her social media pages. And in the days that followed, it became increasingly clear that even celebrities were victims of the body dysmorphic system they had fed over the years. That they too were not perfect, and this ideology they had sold to their fans was now caving in, leaving them in the rubble.

Body dysmorphic disorder (BDD), or body dysmorphia: A mental health condition where a person spends a lot of time worrying about flaws in their appearance.

I remember following this to-and-fro between the Kardashians and the rest of the world. Let me break it down for those who might have a hard time following this story and wonder just who these people are. The Kardashians are the faces behind *Keeping Up with the Kardashians* -a reality show geared at showing fans the glamorous life of this family of five beautiful ladies, their industrious mother, and celebrity father. The show made them famous, earned them millions of dollars, and propelled them to stardom. They are the epitome of what having it all looks like–the looks, the money, the glitz and glam, the social status, the American Dream. They are it. So, for one of them to *actually* look like an average human, well, that was unacceptable.

And I could not help but wonder what this reaction communicated to my son and other teenagers out there. *Was it harming his perception of what he should look like and aspire to be? Was it taking precedence over body acceptance and self-love? Was it so bad to have shadows in your images or (gasps) cellulite on your thighs?* And I was not alone. As I pored through the blogs and watched the countless videos about body dysmorphia, I realized that so many other parents out there were plagued with a similar concern. Had social media doomed our kids to unrealistic expectations of what they should look like?

Why Social Media Could Fuel Your Teen's Body Image

In 15,624 American high school students, thirty percent of males reported a desire to gain weight for muscularity purposes. Around seventeen percent of adolescent boys perceived themselves as underweight, despite the normal weight. Multiracial and African American adolescent boys were nearly two times more likely to attempt weight gain than Caucasian adolescent boys.

In the past, the Kardashians would have overlooked the existence of such a picture. But as time proves, *the internet never forgets*. So, they took legal action rather than stand by and watch people share and repost this unedited picture. They threatened bloggers who dared to post the picture, and within hours, the image was less and less available on the internet. It makes you wonder how far people will go to hide reality from this digital space. Was the proof of an unedited photo too much for the Kardashians to bear? Was this a crack in the otherwise picturesque realm they had shared with their fans? Fans now realized that comparing themselves to what they saw on social media pages was but a farce. Underneath all the good lighting and filters lay a human just like them, facing body image issues.

But that's always been the case with interactions between media and teens. Growing up, I remember seeing all these size two models showcased in magazines. They were small, perky, fit in all the perfect pieces, and seemed to have the world dancing to their tune. So, it was pretty normal that many of my peers wanted to be as small, so petite that they too would make it to these covers. I would see girls starving themselves, thrusting fingers so far down their throats just to ensure no morsel of their lunch made its way to their stomachs -intent on being just the right size. *You are so skinny. Do you even eat? What diet are you on?* These compliments and questions would have them grinning all day long. And don't get me wrong - I was not safe from the pressure either. I also got on diets, even went gluten-free for a year once, avoided carbs -you know the whole thing. All I wanted was that flat stomach, legs for days, and a neck so slim that it complemented every necklace in my mother's wardrobe. And back then, all we had were magazines and TV shows to propel this idea of the perfect body.

But now? It's everywhere! And it affects:

- **The messages teens receive:** Back in my day, we would gaze at models on TV adverts and magazine covers and aspire to be like them. To be poised and placed on a pedestal for all the world to see. And now, teens see these images playing out as young as three. They encounter diet products, weight loss programs, and many messages geared towards selling them towards a *thinner* lifestyle. And what body type is on these ads? Well, *skinny* people–you know, the kind with an apple on their hand and a tape measure on the other, wrapped around their impossibly slim waist. It's not surprising that soon kids become conditioned that thinner is better. After all, they are not seeing products promoting weight gain and higher BMIs. So, even kids as young as five start favoring thinner people, deeming them more socially acceptable, beautiful, and healthier. And it's no surprise that by the time these kids hit ten, a good four in five girls in the US have been on a diet! That's right -kids learn that being *thin* is the way to start attaining this unrealistic goal by the time they are ten.

So, how does social media play into all this? Let's start with the ads. There's not a week that goes by without a weight loss app ad showing up on my screen. I'll be busy minding my business on Instagram, Facebook, or any other app, then bam, a weight loss app! What does such advertising scream to teens? That they need to lose weight!

I came across a wildly disturbing TikTok tend the other day–the *Corpse Bride Diet.* And if the name makes it sound bad, that's because the whole premise behind the diet is quite insane. Well, it turns out that the diet advocates for teens to consume as few calories as possible, mainly surviving on water. The goal?–to be as thin as you can in readiness for the holidays. Add some shaming for anyone who dared to give up on this elusive dream, and that was a recipe for teens to embark on this crazy diet. Oh, and it does not stop there. Investigative journalists uncovered that the social media app's algorithm regularly promoted weight loss content to teens. Within minutes of signing up on the platform, teens are bombarded with countless opinions on how they can start a diet and show the people who have succeeded in doing so. Unfortunately, this implies to teens that their bodies are not good enough, and they need to do more to attain that perfect body.

And TikTok is not the only platform where kids continuously scroll through images and videos of people with what society deems a good body. So, they eventually get drawn closer to the traps of society, seeking to do what it takes to be *thin* or *built* or *lean*.

- **The aspect of validation:** Did you know that most teens double-check before posting an image or video on social media? They question how many likes they will get, how many people will follow them back, how many saves they will get, and so on. So, rather than post what they like, they look for what their peers enjoy. They spend hours poring through similar user feeds to see popular content and choose similar posts. And when they finally post the picture, they gauge their appearance based on how many reactions they get. A poor response rate can be very harmful to a teen's self-image. They think *they are not as attractive as others.*

Sometimes, teens receive negative reactions from rude users, further harming their self-image. When you add the aspect of cyberbullying to this equation, you can see just how fast things can take a turn for the worse. A simple mirror selfie gone wrong could be the reason your kid does not want to leave the house for days. They feel shamed by the world, and to them, their social media world is as much a reality as being in the real world. So, any negative backlash from the faceless pseudo accounts on their profile will hurt them.

So, what happens to kids who are continuously exposed to this unrealistic expectation of perfection? Some fall for it and end up developing unhealthy eating habits. Others suffer low self-esteem, convincing themselves that they are not up to the standard body type. Unfortunately, the effects go deeper than this. Studies show that teens who suffer from body image issues are more likely to feel anxious, depressed, or even commit suicide. Yes, body image issues are that serious.

Living in an Era of Photoshop and Filters

Research has shown that around fifty percent of young thirteen-year-old American girls reported being unhappy with their bodies. This number grew to nearly eighty percent when girls reached seventeen. Nearly eighty percent of young teenage girls report fears of becoming fat.

Do you want to know an interesting bit about the unedited Khloe photo? Most people preferred it over the hundreds of other heavily edited posts on her Instagram page. Here she was, a real woman, with a beautiful and conventional body type–something relatable and attainable. But rather than post this, she would prefer to work on her pictures. Why?

Well, Khloe is not the only one who edits her photos. Many teenagers do the same thing–they call it filters. You may have even used some of these effects in your photos. Gone are the days when we adjusted for lighting and contrast. Now, you can create a whole other face using an app!

Don't like the freckles on your face? You can hide them.

Tired of the marks on your neck? Filter them!

Want to appear curvier? There's an app for that!

So, does this ability to alter our appearances help or hurt our teens? Let's see what the recent studies have to say about this:

- **The rise of digital beauty:** The current digital apps allow you to alter everything about yourself–your nose, skin color, eye size, smile, *literally* everything. So, if you don't like it, you can change it! The result? People are becoming more attached to these altered images they capture of themselves. Plastic surgeons have even claimed that people come to them with pictures of these enhanced images and say they want to look like that. They want augmentation that matches what they post on social media. Oh, and it's obsessive. It starts with the eyes, then moves to the nose, then down to the cheekbones, and it never stops–because achieving a perfect face is impossible. Even celebs who post perfect images have edited these pictures–so people are engaging in a wild goose chase.

- **The increase in comparison:** It's quite normal to encounter someone you've seen on social media and not recognize who they are. Why? Because the original images hardly ever live up to the retouched ones. And those who filter their images know this and are cast into a body dysmorphic state, feeling conscious of their true selves–feeling like the original images are not good enough -losing their confidence. Unfortunately, this is a step closer to a dissociative disorder–the inability to connect with the original image instead of feeling connected with the retouched one. So, a teenager ends up falling deeper into the ensnares of digital beauty, unable to accept the perceived imperfections they see when they don't have filters.

So, while it might seem like your teen is just having fun with filters, it could boil down to much deeper self-image issues. And of course, the more they see these airbrushed celeb and influencer images, the more inclined they will be to touch up their pictures. Now, am I saying that all social media influence is terrible? Not at all. Body positivity has gained traction over the years, emphasizing that **all bodies are beautiful**. With body-positive role models like Lizzo and Demi Lovato sharing their journeys on self-love, teens can get inspired to realize their bodies are perfect as they are. And ease up on all the filtering.

Does Your Teen Have an Eating Disorder?

In German Adolescent girls, nearly one-third perceived a BMI of less than eighteen to be the ideal female body size. Thirty-six percent of German child/adolescent girls felt fat, twenty-two percent were terrified of gaining weight, and thirty-six percent reported regularly feeling upset about their weight or shape.

Amid the controversy surrounding the unedited photo, Khloe was quick with an answer. According to the celebrity, she had suffered body dysmorphia all her life. Growing up in a family with four other girls, she often suffered a backlash regarding her appearance. People had called her fat. Others had alluded that she was the ugly one. Some had even gone as far as insinuating that she must have a different father from her other sisters. So, she took control of the situation by perfecting her pictures. She pointed out that choosing what to share was no longer what she wanted to be judged on. But, of course, this explanation only brought on more scrutiny.

But we could all see where she was coming from–nobody wants to be labeled fat or ugly or the black sheep in the family. Society is rarely kind to those it feels do not meet its standards. So, unbeknownst to you, your child may go through a struggle with their body image–and they might have resulted in starving themselves, going on crash diets, or even developed bulimic habits. All these are forms of eating disorders. Unfortunately, I have learned that when people hear of eating disorders, their minds go to starving kids. But it can also take the opposite route. Below are the categories:

- **Anorexia:** Your kid wants to be thin, cannot stand gaining weight, and thinks they are fat even with bones sticking out of their skin. So, to remain slim, they starve themselves and go on diets just to consume as few calories as possible.

- **Bulimia:** Your kid seems to eat well. They eat a lot of food at once. Then, they try to eliminate the calories at once–by exercising too much, using laxatives, throwing up, etc. You might not even know that your kid is bulimic because they will not lose too much weight and will almost always join you for dinner.

- **BED (Binge Eating Disorder):** Your teen will often binge on a lot of junk food even when they are satisfied. They gain weight because they don't eliminate the calories like bulimics.

- **EDNOS (Eating Disorders Not Otherwise Specified):** If your teen has an eating disorder that does not meet the above specifications, their relationship with food could fall into this category.

How can you tell that they have gone down this rabbit hole? You assess if:

- **Their eating habits have changed.** They:
  - Suddenly prefer eating alone or in secret.

- Seem to overeat at once.
- Are very specific about how they eat–perhaps they only use a particular bowl or count their calories too much.
- Want to cook for the family but barely touch what they make.
- Often go to the loo after eating (you may have heard them making themselves sick).
- Consume a lot of food yet maintain a 'normal' weight.
- Have an unhealthy attitude about food and often feel guilty about eating, appear stressed during mealtimes, or avoid mealtimes.
- Avoid eating in public.
- Stash food in their rooms.

- **Their overall demeanor has changed.** They now:
  - Prefer wearing baggy clothes as if they are hiding their bodies.
  - Have this urge to check their weight regularly and care so much about how much they weigh.
  - Are distancing themselves from their peers.

- Weigh significantly more or significantly less than they should at their age and height (typically, they should gain weight throughout adolescence).
- Care so much about what others think of their bodies.

- **Are showing any of these physical signs?** They:
- Are often tired.
- Have dry skin.
- Have swollen cheeks.
- Often feel cold.
- Complain of stomach aches.
- Faint often or complain of dizziness.
- Have mouth infections or sensitive teeth.
- Suffer bad breath, or
- Have scars on their fingers.

- **Appear psychologically distressed and show signs of**:
- Depression
- Anxiety
- Low self-esteem
- Insomnia
- Irritability
- Suicidal impulses

Have you noticed any of these changes in your teen? You should not ignore them. While we would like to think that the symptoms will pass, that's not always the case. And what may seem like a small phase could turn into a depressive or suicidal stage for your teen. It's important to talk to your kid about what they are going through and ask if everything is okay. We keep coming back to the chapter on communication. If your teen won't talk to you, encourage them to speak to someone they trust or get them into therapy. We will also get into how you could play a part in their body image issues.

Is Social Media to Blame for the Rise in Eating Disorders?

Sure, algorithms that direct our kids to weight loss challenges and apps are not helping matters. But even before social media, eating disorders still existed–I know that my unhealthy relationship with food did not start when the internet was invented. It started much earlier than that. So, while social media may fuel this constant need to be perfect, your teen's relationship with food may result from:

- A close family member or friend suffering from an eating disorder.

- Battling a mental health problem like anxiety.
- Being in a career or hobby that requires them to be thin, e.g., dancing.
- Cyberbullying and even physical bullying.
- Social pressures from peers, family members, etc.
- A history of abuse.
- Undergoing stressful events.

The cause of eating disorders is not always easy to pinpoint. But with a supportive home base and professional mental help to boot, your teen develops a healthy relationship with their body and food. Unfortunately, like with most mental disorders, eating disorders do not just go away–they linger. It takes a lot of work to help your teen get to a place where they can feel comfortable in their bodies. So, how can we play a part in this?

How to Nurture a Healthy Body Image in Teenagers

In 657 Spanish girls, nearly fifty percent expressed a desire for a thinner body, despite being of average body weight. In the same sample of Spanish girls, almost ninety percent of overweight girls expressed a desire for a thinner body. Only eleven percent wanted their body to stay the same.

Fans were happy with Khloe being open about body dysmorphia -some hadn't even known the term existed- a scientific way to describe their struggles with body image issues. Still, they were not satisfied with her reaction. If she was fighting against body shaming, why was she putting out these highly edited photos? Why was she perpetuating a problem she admitted existed and one that was eroding the confidence of millions of people in the world? Why was she feeding the system? Some may argue that this was her way of seeking a safe space in an otherwise cruel digital world. But was there another way to deal with her dysmorphia? Well, that's a question better posed to Khloe.

So, amidst all this debate about filtering images, Photoshop, and faking it till you make it, can we cultivate a healthy body image in teens? The good news is that we can. But how?

- **Being positive:** Teens spend all day around people who quickly point out their flaws. For example, *that dress does not suit your body type. Your forehead is too big to pull off that look.* So, having a positive reminder about their attributes goes a long way in building their confidence. Remind them they are beautiful and that their bodies are works of wonder. *Look at what a good job you did with your hands! What a pleasant voice you have!*

- **Not teasing them:** Your teen is probably already having it rough on social media. And even if they are not, they are highly emotional and will not take well to teasing, even the good-natured kind. So, don't start talking about *how much weight they have gained,* or *they are so thin that the wind could blow them away.* They already know if they have gained or lost weight–cut it out with the teasing.

- **Encouraging positive self-talk:** Sometimes, we are our biggest critics. So, your teen might be too hard on themselves in how they think about their bodies. Teach them to love their bodies by appreciating what they can do for them. Don't point out the vain things like *you have a smooth face.* Instead, go deeper and teach them to appreciate functionality like *with these hands, I can paint,* or *my legs allow me to run across the track.*

- **Talking about the social media influence:** We can't live as if social media does not exist. So, talking to our teens is the way out. First, ask your child what they think about the messages relayed on these platforms. How do they make them feel? Then talk about why ads are formulated to make us feel like we need something that the marketer can give us. That is why weight loss apps sell so much because they trigger us to feel bad about our weight–and then we buy into this marketing ploy. Teach your child to assess these marketing gimmicks and understand each ad's reasoning.

- Please talk about the influence of filters and how these can alter our self-worth. Add that the idea of perfection is fleeting because nobody is perfect. And show them the beauty in accepting one's body as it is.

- **Watching how you talk:** You may have noticed that your kid has an eating disorder. They are eating too little, too much, infrequently, all the time, you name it. Instead of chiding them about it or resorting to nagging, hold back and encourage the whole family to make healthy decisions. For example, rather than serve cake for dessert, offer fruit juice. Instead of sitting all weekend and binge-watching series, take everyone out for a walk. When teens are active and have the whole family participating, they focus less on food and more on the activities. Ensure they don't feel singled out, as this can worsen their relationship with food. Instead, make it a family thing.

- **Staying active:** Physical activity does wonders for a teen's mental health. So, find something they enjoy doing–swimming, cycling, dancing, running, skateboarding–anything that helps them release more endorphins. Even if they may not be great at it, this bust of activity makes them feel better about themselves and much more confident. And the effect lasts longer than a filter.

- **Encouraging good friendships:** You are the average of the five people closest to you. So, if your teen hangs out with people who are obsessed with their self-image, the effect can get to them. Encourage them to branch out and seek connections with other people who may positively affect them.

Don't forget to debunk the myth that beautiful people are happy. Sometimes, teens think that all their problems will disappear if they are attractive, and everyone will like them. Remind them that while being beautiful is a perk, it does not take away life's struggles. So, if they are escaping an issue by pursuing the perfect body, they are better off dealing with the real problem. And show them how they can deal with their problems head-on healthily.

Why It Starts with You: Being the Role Model for Your Teenager

In over 50,000 adults, sixty percent of women thought they were too heavy and self-conscious about their weight, thirty percent reported being too uncomfortable in a swimsuit, and twenty percent thought they were unattractive.

Besides Khloe, many other celebrities have talked about their struggles with body image. Examples include Reid Ewing, Shirley Manson, Robert Patterson, Andy Warhol, and Sylvia Plath. Billie Eilish, a sensational hit with the Gen Zs, admitted, *"I've never felt comfortable in really tiny clothes. I was always worried about my appearance. That was the peak of my body dysmorphia. I couldn't look in the mirror at all."*

These are but a fraction of the people who understand what it feels like to want your body to be something it's not.

To look in the mirror and feel unhappy about what you see.

To live life hoping and wishing to be in another body.

Forever escaping the reality that exists and wallowing in what could have been. And as much as we would like to blame mainstream media for perpetuating these unrealistic body images on our kids, have we played a part in it? Could you be the reason your child is unhappy with their body?

Well, have you considered:

- **How compassionate are you towards yourself?** Studies show that kind parents often have a positive body image that they pass down to their kids.

- **What do you say about other people's bodies?** While you might be keen on teaching your kid to love themselves, they will hear what you say about others. So, if you make snide comments about other people's bodies, your kid will know that your ***all bodies are beautiful*** campaign is hogwash.

- **What do you say about your body?** Self-criticism sometimes creeps upon us. But doing it in front of our kids only communicates the notion that a perfect body exists. When you gain a few pounds and say that *you feel fat* or get a zit and say *you look ugly*, you imply falling below a standard. And your kid picks it up. So, when they gain weight or have a rash, and you tell them they are beautiful, the double standard will be evident.

- **How do you treat your body?** A healthy body image also stems from how you handle your body. Do you eat well, exercise, sleep enough, and hydrate? Kids learn from their parents. So, if they see you putting effort into caring for your body, they emulate this, acknowledging the benefits of doing so.

- **The media you consume.** Sure, you can point out all that's wrong with filtered images and weight loss challenges. But are you following such trends on social media? Are you jumping at the chance to buy fat loss pills or getting on two-week shred diets? Are you walking the talk you are so fervently passing down to your child? What you read, watch, and buy also sends a message to your child.

So, look in the mirror before you point fingers at celebrities and talk about how they have corrupted young minds. Are you guilty of perpetuating these societal standards? Is there anything you can do about it? Remember that *charity begins at home. It starts with you.*

***

Chapter Thirteen

Keeping Up With The Jenners

"I smoked my first cigarette when I was eleven. I didn't want to. But all my friends were smoking, and I didn't want to be out of the group. Once I'd started, I couldn't stop. I was addicted... I wish I hadn't started. I knew it was wrong, and I didn't want to." –
Mike, Sixteen-year-old

Do you remember when keeping up with the Joneses was the *in* thing? Well, social media changed that! Now, kids are not just keeping up with their neighbors -they are also trying to keep up with the whole world. And if what I've seen in the past few months is an indicator of what is coming, parents cannot stand by and watch. Why? Well, standing out of the crowd now requires kids to be on top of all social media challenges. Forget about when smoking a cigarette behind the class during recess was the height of peer pressure. Now, kids have to do many things on social media to remain relevant and hold on to their friends. So, if they are not doing the #cratechallenge, they are jumping on the #corpsebridediet challenge, and the list continues. But why is this a problem?

Well, like I said, standing out is becoming much harder. So, the challenges are getting crazier by the day. I came across one called the #blackoutchallenge. The premise?– hold your breath until you pass out due to lack of oxygen. And the results? At the time of writing this book, at least eighty kids had passed on, attempting the challenge. The deaths were not enough to keep kids from playing this game–because that's what it is to them. So, the CDC released a list of signs to help parents single out any kids actively taking part in the game. That's how important being socially relevant is to some kids–how vital those likes, comments, and reactions are. They are even willing to face the prospect of dying.

So, parents cannot assume that their kids are hurdled inside a car smoking or simply sneaking drinks at parties.

The social media era has taken peer pressure to a whole other level–peer pressure is now viral and gets to your teen even in the confines of their room.

Out With the Joneses and In with the Jenners

"My peer group wants to make a difference. We are all doing well at school, and we want to keep it that way. We know there are bad things out there, and we want to help each other make the right decisions." –
Brad, Seventeen-year-old

When *Keeping Up with the Kardashians* graced our screens, the reactions were quite varied. Some people could not help but catch each episode, marveling at these beautiful women who seemed to have it all. And then some dismissed the show, terming it as unrealistic and whatnot. Regardless of where people stood, the show was a hit and raked in millions of dollars for the main characters. Then Instagram, Snapchat, Facebook, and the likes hit the scene. And guess what? The popularity of the Kardashians carried over to these social media platforms, with each garnering tens of millions of followers. These fans could not believe their luck, as they got a front-row seat to the glamorous lives of these reality stars. And guess who your teen probably looks up to now? The Kendall Jenner of this world–the supermodels or the Kylie Jenner of social media–the fashionable business gurus who never have a hair out of place. Even if they are not keenly following the Jenners, they are following the crop of socialites and influencers who gained from the rise of the Kardashians — your Natalie Halcros, Nikita Draguns, Paris Hilton, and the list goes on. These are the people whose lives continuously flash their lifestyles on social media for all to see. But how has this changed teenagerhood?

- **It's changed their source of validation:** Teens rarely know who they are, so they often seek validation from their peers. They experiment, try out different personas, and decide what works for them best. Remember that stage when you were still trying to see which shoe fit? Teens now do it in the full glare of social media. As they try to see what works, they try many things that can be risky, like the #blackoutchallenge. And that's not all– they also attach their feelings of self-worth to the reception they get on social media. If their accounts take off and garner many views, fans, comments, and likes, they exalt themselves. After all, their favorite stars, who people think the world about, are also garnering high numbers. But if their numbers are low, self-criticism often follows. They feel that if strangers don't appreciate them; it says something about their likeability, appearance, etc. Add the fact that cyberbullying is on the rise. That means that a faceless person can key in some harsh words and send your teen spiraling in a dismal state. It's a double-edged sword.

- **The grasp on reality has reduced:** Teens are no longer just comparing their lives to those of their peers in school and at home. A teen in Australia can keep up with what another in Canada or Mexico is doing. And people post the perfect side of their life – the clothes, the parties, the grades, the friends, etc. So, teens are now faced with the pressure to be as perfect as these other teens and influencers *living their best lives*. That means that on top of doing their homework and carving out their path to college, they also have the added pressure to have a thriving social media presence. Oh, and they should only show the fun stuff because that's what their followers want to see. So, they get to show just a bit of who they are for fear of losing their following – changing who they are for the likes and comments.

- **The level of competition is higher now:** With Kylie Jenner packing $5,000 mini bags on casual hangouts and Natalie Halcro launching hundreds of dollars worth of swimsuits, teens have it cut out for them. And let's get into the teens launching businesses worth millions of dollars, starting killer YouTube channels, succeeding in online spaces, and elbowing their way out of the crowd. To digital teens, fitting in is no longer about getting in with the cool kids. It's now about having the latest haircut, the new car brand, the finest cut of jeans, the next-level skincare products–this rat race never ends. And, of course, teens must strive to keep showing that they have what it takes. If they can prove that they are doing well on social media, they can believe it. That's where the whole *faking it till you make it* mantra comes in–otherwise, they are dead to the world. That's how serious fitting in is in the digital era.

In the last chapter, we also talked about how social media has shaped body image in teens in this digital age. So, as your teen navigates the changes in the peer pressure scope, it's easy to see how they would feel lost in all of it. Yes, they still face the usual pressure of doing drugs, having sex, sexting, and breaking the rules. But now, they need to do it on a much broader scale to stand a chance of having any social credit. Can you see how hard that would be?

Para-social Relationships in the Digital Age

> *"My friends are like family to me, and we all look out for each other. It's what keeps me calm 'cause I need them to support me when I need help. I'm there for them when they need me to. It's cool, and it works."*
> –**Brad, Seventeen-year-old**

Do you know why influencers are on the rise? Well, people crave the lifestyles they exude and live up to these personas. And that leads to the development of para-social relationships, which are, in fact, one-sided relationships. The influencer shares their life — what they eat, their family, their hobbies, and so on. And a fan on the other side connects with this lifestyle, embracing it, and feeling like they understand this influence. So, the fan thinks of the influencer as a friend.

Para-social relationships exist not only between fans and influencers. They also exist between fans and movie stars, animated characters, fictional characters, media hosts, etc.

The thing here is that one person gives, and the other takes, and that's all there is to it. I'll give you the example of my sixteen-year-old niece, who was once obsessed with an influencer. The influencer would rave about a new exercise regimen, and my niece would start it the following week. If the said influencer started a new diet, so would my niece. She even influenced the sports my niece watched, the movies she liked, the snacks she ate–my niece thought of this person as a best friend. And if we tried to tell her that the relationship was not real, she would burst into tears or get angry. She later went through her para-social breakup with this influencer when she got an actual best friend.

But it left us wondering, why would someone form a relationship with someone they barely know? Well, there's the fact that humans are social. So, we are always open to interacting with other people. Then there's the connection aspect–we all crave to establish a relationship with someone who *gets us.* And when we get a media personality who checks this box, idealizing them is normal–it's been the case for decades. And for a long time, these relationships have helped to influence purchasing behaviors. Brands would use athletes and celebs to push their products, and it worked. It later became apparent that these relationships also boiled down to political, social, and economic decisions.

Has that changed in the digital age? Not even close– these relationships have only become stronger. Relationships with social media personalities occur in real-time. So, a celebrity can like, comment on, retweet, respond to, or even message a fan on the platform. The possibility of this link-up encourages more people to reach out to their favorite stars on these platforms. Also, stars share more about their lives now, creating this illusion of friendship with their fans. Their fans feel like they know them and feel seen and heard.

Is it a good thing? Sure, for those years that my niece followed the said influencer, she had a sense of direction. And luckily, it was a positive one -she ate better, exercised more, paid more attention to her studies, and upped her fashion game. But of course, this was the positive side of these relationships–when people use para-social interactions as a bonus to their existing relationships. So, can these relationships take a sour turn? Sure!–When people choose to replace or replicate existing relationships with these online personas. Or when these relationships stem from depression, anxiety, and negative experiences from relationships with real people. In these cases, the reasons behind the connection could pave the way for a negative para-social relationship. The fan, in this case, can be easily manipulated into engaging in harmful behavior like the #blackedoutchallenge. So, if your teen goes looking for validation or a connection in the online space, you can't be sure who they will choose to emulate. Thus, you need to question who they follow and what traits they like in these personas.

Who are Your Teenager's Friends?

*"I started doing drugs when I was fifteen. All my friends were into it, and I honestly felt it was ok to do the stuff with them. I now know that I shouldn't have done it, and it has taken me over a year to get back to where I'm at today. I've got drugs out of my body. I still don't feel good about it, and some days can be better than others, but I'm looking forward, not backward." –**Alison, Eighteen-year-old**

Now that we know we have to look out for real and para-social friends, how can you ensure your teen makes the right choice? It all starts by asking yourself key questions about these people. These are:

- **What do they want for themselves?** Do your teen's friends have any clue what they want to do when they finish high school? What are their ambitions? While their friends may not have a strategic plan in place, you can tell if they are hopeful about what lies ahead. And that makes all the difference between someone who pushes your kid forward or holds them back.

- **What do they spend their free time doing?** Are they out playing sports, volunteering, spending time with family, hanging out at the mall, trying new hobbies, etc.? Or do their fun activities gear towards trying the latest crazy Tiktok trends, partying, sneaking out, and other negative activities?

- **Who are their influences?** Get to know where your teen friends hang out, their family and social lives, where they go to school, and other aspects of their environment that could shape them. Are these influences you want around your child? Of course, kids do not choose all their circumstances. But where they have a choice, are you happy with their decisions?

- **What does your teen think of their friends?** Genuine admiration, love, and respect are all good signs that your teen is in a balanced relationship. But what if their friendships leave them feeling jealous because they look up to these friends? Well, that points to an imbalance with your teen on the losing end, putting them at risk of negative peer pressure. And the opposite also holds. If your teen views their friends as minions or people who need help, that puts too much work on their shoulders. Bullying or encouraging dependency issues are just as bad as falling in with a rough crowd.

These questions also apply to your teen's favorite influencers. Are they impacting them positively? Why does your teen like these influencers? Are they sacrificing genuine relationships in favor of these parasocial interactions?

It might feel like you are prying into your child's life, but doing so could help you gauge just who influences your child. Keep in mind that teens lean more on peer influence during adolescence than on parental advice. So, if they are spending time with questionable people or following them on social media, they could be in *actual* danger.

Signs That Your Teenager is Under Peer Pressure

"I think that's important. I know it was peer pressure that got me into that stuff. We all got screwed up. My advice to anyone is if you know you shouldn't do stuff, then don't do it–even if your friends think it's cool. It's not worth it, and your life gets messed up. I still have some of my friends, but they've changed. They're still trying to get their lives together. Don't do drugs. You only get one body, and only you can look after it." –Alison, Eighteen-year-old

Let's start by differentiating the types of peer pressure. There's the good kind – the type that pushes you to do and be better. My niece, for example, became a better person by following a positive influence. Eventually, she grew out of her cocoon and ventured into the real world, confident in her new skills. Then there's the negative kind – the one we group under the umbrella known as peer pressure. It's the kind that has your teen sending nudes to strangers, sexting, drinking alcohol, smoking, and doing all sorts of things on social media. So, you can see that peer pressure is not all bad. It can be good. But for now, let's focus on how you can gauge if your kid has embraced the negative side of peer pressure:

- **They change their behavior around certain people.** Your kid acts a particular way around you, and as soon as they are with their friends, they are a whole different person. That's a sign right there.

- **They often talk about not fitting in and seem concerned about it.** Maybe they are in a new school and haven't made any new friends because they are not cool enough. Or have friends in higher social circles who shun them, leaving them feeling left out. This isolation can push them to hang out with the wrong crowd.

- **They are always trying new things, some of which you may not agree with.** It's normal for teens to change the way they dress or do their hair or even where they hang out–that's all part of experimenting. But what if you get a whiff of marijuana when they walk past you or find an empty beer bottle in the trash can? That could be a sign that your teen is trying drugs with their friends.

- **They suddenly seem interested in a new way of dressing that appears completely different from who they are.** Teens always want to try new things. But sometimes, this curiosity or interest could lie in negative peer pressure. Maybe their friends are now buying designer items, and they feel the need to keep up. Or they want to dress like influencers they see on social media. Sometimes, it's a beneficial influence. But it's not a good sign if they are buying things you would not approve of or are bleeding their accounts dry just to buy these things.

- **They compare themselves unhealthily.** We have all admired other people, even I do it. I'll see someone post that they were up by 5 am every day, and I will respect the work they put into this consistency. But I don't beat myself up about it. But your teen may not have grasped this notion of healthy comparison. So, when they see someone with something they wish they had, they wish they have what that person has. The result?–they can start acting like this other person, hoping to take what they have.

- **They blame other people for their behavior.** You find your teen not doing the right thing, and they are fast to state that *they did not want to do it. Their friends made them do it.* Well, this signifies that even if your teen knows what's right and wrong, their willpower to say no is highly influenced by who is around them.

- **They make a conscious effort not to excel so much**. I have seen bright kids whose grades have suffered because they thought being smart was too nerdy. Or skipped school just to avoid looking like a stickler for rules. I know someone who intentionally missed an athletic competition because his friends felt he was too much of a high achiever. So yes, negative peer pressure could send your kid down a path of self-sabotage. They want to fit in so badly that they hurt themselves and their future.

Have you seen any of these signs in your kids? Interestingly, some kids will show none of these signs. So, if you can't tell if anything is amiss, how about inviting your teen's friends over for lunch? - Or taking them out to the mall? You can see how your teen relates to them and use this as the baseline. Also, to figure out an influencer's effect on them, how about following that influencer and seeing what kind of content they put out there?

Helping Your Teen Cope with Social Pressures

"I like cars a lot. My friends and I started stealing cars over a year ago. I didn't want to do it, but we all felt we could have fun and get away with it. I've been

caught twice by the cops, and they say if I do this again, I will go to jail." –Ryan, Fifteen-year-old

Peers are important to us, but that's not to say that those connections come easily–even as adults, we still somehow juggle these relationships. And almost every week, I listen to a podcast or come across a blog with someone talking about issues in friendships. So, to expect our kids to manage these links with no help would put quite a load on their backs. Here is how you can help your child navigate the ins and outs of peer relationships without falling in with the wrong crowd:

- **Please communicate with your child:** Chapter five keeps revisiting us for a good reason. Who can your child turn to when they feel pushed to be a different person from who they are? Do they come to you and say *all my friends are trying alcohol this weekend and I am not sure I want to do it,* or do they struggle with it alone? If you can open the communication lines, your child will probably come to you when they lose what to do.

- **Help them build confidence:** I was watching Gilmore Girls the other day when I noticed how Lorelai had brought up this confident and intelligent young girl. While I know that it's highly fictional, I could not help but see the truth in her daughter's stance on so many societal issues. And do you know which kid can stand up to a group of popular kids and refuse to join their clique? A confident child, that's who! Enhance your teen's confidence in who they are so they can choose what's best for them. Praise them when they do what's right and be there for them when they need that extra motivation. While I am not saying that Gilmore Girls is the new benchmark for raising confident children, it did not miss the mark either.

- **Teach them self-compassion:** In chapter twelve, we talked about this when covering body image issues. When teens have compassion for themselves, they are less likely to fall into negative friendships.

- **Teach them how to say no:** It's easy to tell your teen to say *no* when they don't want to do something. But picture this. Your child is at a party, and someone pushes a cigarette their way and asks them to take a puff. Do they just say *"no,"* or can they say no to help them save face? Maybe they could go, *"No, I don't like the smell."* Can you think of other scenarios and how your child can get out of them? You can have fun role-playing with your kid to help them prepare for that moment. Maybe you can even come up with a secret code. They can text you in the heat of the moment, and you can call them with some made-up emergency.

- **Encourage positive peer pressure:** I stated that not all peer pressure is bad. Some of it is so good that your child is better off with it in their life. For example, people who advocate for mental health, body positivity, mindfulness, sound financial practices, etc., are people your kid would benefit from following. So, please encourage your child to embrace such positivity and broaden their social networks. Sometimes, kids fall into the wrong company because they don't have options. But with a thriving offline life, they will have an easier time staying on the right track.

Like with most teen topics, this is one you will need to cover continuously. But rather than make it a mundane one-way conversation, make it fun. Get to know your teen's favorite influencers and strike up conversations about what they are up to. Then your teen can even unknowingly let you in on what their real-life friends have been doing, and you can gauge if any red flags are showing.

Practicing What You Preach

"I don't like what this has done to my mom and dad. They don't want me to hang with these guys anymore, but they're my friends. I wouldn't do this on my own, but when I'm with the guys, it makes me feel good, and I can do stuff." –Ryan, Fifteen-year-old

The whole d#% world is just as obsessed with who's the best dressed and who's having #$%

Who gets the money?

Who gets the honies?

Who's kind of cute?

And who's just a mess?

Those are a few lines off *High School Never Ends,* a song that resonates with me till now. It discusses how Brad Pitt plays the quarterback and Bill Gates is on the chess team. It even gets to how the car you drive matters, regardless of being sixteen or thirty-five. And you know what? It's true–peer pressure does not end at adolescence–some people struggle to fit in decades after high school.

So, before you question your child's decisions, maybe it's time you asked yourself if:

- Your offline friends have a beneficial influence on you, and
- Your favorite influencers impact you positively.

Your kid learns from you. That means that if you are always doing things because you care *what other people will say or do*, then you can't expect your child to foster a different mindset. They will also care what others say because if it's good enough for you, then it should be sufficient for them.

So, go through the same questions you would ask your child about their friends and use them to assess your circle. Are they a good reflection of your choices? Do you exhibit any signs of suffering from negative peer pressure? Then look at ways you can wane yourself off this pressure and, if need be, seek therapy. Some trenches we dig ourselves into require us to reach for help to claw ourselves out–and admitting that you might have some questionable friends might be the way to start.

***

Chapter Fourteen

Substance Abuse In Teenagers

I awoke to every mother's nightmare. I found my twenty–year–old son dead in his bed of an accidental heroin and valium overdose.

The excerpts in this section detail the moments that led to the demise of a young man who had his whole life before him. In chapter nine, do you remember Joy -The depressed teen who seemed to have it all going for them yet was secretly battling suicidal thoughts? This young man was a lot like this, so his parents did not even know they were losing him until it was too late.

Why? Well, he was a model child–excelling in his own right in his academic and extracurricular activities. He had a thriving social life, got into just enough trouble for a teen, and was what most parents would describe as a typical teen. But behind this almost perfect facade, he had a lot of pain coursing through his being.

So, he sought refuge in the drugs and hid it so well that even his parents, who shared a roof with him, could not see what was happening. And they had no reason to question his behavior because the usual pain points were missing–he was good in school, well-behaved, and well-liked. These were not the makings of drug addicts, but he was one. Eventually, he started showing signs he was not doing too well–but these signs were relatively scanty and not the kind most parents expect. So, he made do with deception, and the crumbs he was leaving for his loved ones went unnoticed– such that by the time he was struggling, he was doing hard drugs. Unfortunately, he did not make it and passed on at the tender age of twenty.

As painful as it is, this true story sheds even more light on why we cannot stand back and hope that drug abuse is but a phase that our kids can grow out of. My deepest condolences go out to anyone who has suffered the loss of a loved one at the hands of drugs.

Why Teens Think Drugs are Cool

He was a promising college student with everything to live for. He was bright, athletic, popular, and handsome -his family and many friends dearly loved him. Drugs destroyed his life.

The young man in this story did not start doing drugs at twenty. Like most teens, he began by experimenting with various drugs at a young age. In the eighth grade, it started with tobacco and marijuana -you know how most kids are. They think these drugs are harmless–just something to make the moments more fun. But they were not. They were gateways to much harder drugs in the years that followed. So when he was twenty and in college, he got his first taste of heroin in the company of two friends–just a few boys trying to see what the fuss was about. One of his friends got ill, and the other ran scared. But for our young man? The love was almost instantaneous–he *liked* how he felt after taking the drug. And that established what was to be a long struggle as he tried to free himself from something that was destroying him–something he had to hide from those he loved.

As a parent reading this, you might wonder what would push a teen to even experiment with drugs. What would propel them to embark on a journey that could end their life? Unfortunately, I cannot pinpoint a single reason that could get your child to that point. Why? Because the reasons are not always as obvious. Teens can do drugs because:

- **Drugs are available:** Do you know how easy it is to access drugs? They are everywhere–in movies, social media, our homes, parties, malls, you name it! So, imagine being a teen surrounded by friends who occasionally smoke or drink. Or you come from a home where alcohol is always available. Wouldn't you be at a high risk of experimentation? Let's not leave out the online influence either–teens who idealize people who often abuse drugs will probably emulate these negative behaviors.

- **They are anxious:** Have you ever noticed how people suddenly lose their inhibitions when they are high? The shy guy in the corner now becomes the life of the party, somehow blending in with everyone. That's the effect of drugs – they make people feel confident and enable them to escape the reality of their anxiety. So, when an anxious teen gets a hit of that drug-induced courage, you can imagine how relieving it must feel – an answer to their social anxiety or any other anxiety. And they take the drugs, deeming them to be the easy way out and not knowing just how rough the road ahead can be.

- **They are curious:** Teens are at the helm of exploration. They want to know how everything feels. *What is it like to get high?* And how do they get to know?–not by reading books or watching movies. It's by sneaking that beer or smoking that blunt. Or even accepting that random pill at a party–*just to see what it's all about.*

- **They want to have fun:** Some people think parties or even road trips are not fun when sober. And teens are not different. They grow up in a world that idealizes drunken stupors that end up in walks of shame or crazy drunken escapades. And they think that this makes parties, festivals, and even life fun. So, it's not unusual for teens to use drugs just for the aspect of *fun*.

- **They want to self-medicate:** Does your teen have a sound support system? Sometimes, the overwhelming need to destress can get to them. They have homework piling up, extracurricular activities to show up to, friends to hang out with, and a social media presence to polish up for that social cred. We haven't even added the need to help in the house, take care of their mental health, eat well, work out, and deal with the usual goings-on in their lives. Without a point of release, the pressure can build up to unhealthy levels, and they may think that the way out is to get high.

- **They want to rebel:** We've talked about the undeveloped prefrontal cortex in most parts of this book. Your teen is no longer a child, and they want to know that you understand this. If they feel you are pushing back on their growth, emotional outbursts are not the only way to react. Some take to drugs *just* to prove that they are adults–by doing something thought to be only for adults. It's them grasping for the last straw available to them–a fight for independence.

- **They don't know any better:** What do most parents tell their teens about drugs? Here's an example: *drugs will kill you.* This statement might seem right. After all, so many people have succumbed to the effects of drugs. But not everyone who takes drugs goes down this path. And your teen probably knows a highly successful person who does drugs and seems to do great. So, why would they believe such a statement? They would likely believe their friend, who says *even X, has been taking marijuana for ten years and has now launched a* *million-dollar app.* Thus, feeding our teens with partial or false facts can push them closer to doing drugs.

Can you see why it's easy for your teen to fall into the traps of drug abuse? While they might not be facing peer pressure to do drugs or partying every weekend in clubs, they could seek drugs for other reasons. Maybe their anxiety has gotten to them, or they want to show you how *big* they have become. Or they saw X doing drugs on social media and now think it looks so cool that they too must get some in their system. It's never just obvious, and that's what makes teen drug abuse so rampant and dangerous.

What Drugs *Actually* Do to Teenagers

He started using tobacco and marijuana in the eighth grade. He was in denial about the problem, minimizing it, as so many young people do. I was unaware that he was using drugs, thinking the changes <u>were just adolescent behavior.</u>

We've all heard about the potential effects of doing drugs. Some are true, some are skewed, and others are deliberately exaggerated. So, what's the truth? What befalls the teens who do drugs?

- **Their emotions suffer:** While some teens use drugs to mask their emotional turmoil, drugs can have the opposite effect. They will help your teen feel better in the moment. But in the long run, they worsen the emotional problems. Why?–because your teen does not deal with what's disturbing them. So, if your teen is dealing with depression, they will develop drugs dependence. And the side effects and withdrawal symptoms will only push them deeper into their dark emotional state. Studies also show that teens who abuse drugs are at a higher risk of developing anxiety or depression.

- **Their behaviors change:** Teens who abuse drugs often engage in deception, aggression, and theft. Your teen suddenly starts behaving out of character. They seem or are verbally or physically aggressive and often engage in fights. Or resort to illegal activities to raise cash to buy drugs, including stealing from you or selling their possessions. So, you deal with problems you had not encountered in the past. Suddenly, your neighbors and teen's teachers seem to have a bone to pick with your child. And even you can't deny that they have changed for the worse.

- **They develop a substance dependence:** Teens are still in the developmental stages, and their brains are very *impressionable,* if I may say so. That means that once they use drugs, the likelihood of developing an addiction is high. They get used to getting that *high* and escaping from reality. And unfortunately, such teens can relapse later in life and still fall into the snares of drugs.

- **They engage in risky sex:** We talked about how important it is to speak to our children about *the birds and the bees.* But you know what would derail this progress?–drug abuse. Teens doing drugs often lose their inhibitions and cross lines they otherwise would not have. They find themselves in bed with strangers and are more likely to contract STDs, get sexually abused, or even fall pregnant or impregnate someone. And the guilt, shame, or trauma that follows such events can worsen their drug abuse.

- **Their grades suffer:** Teens who abuse drugs suffer short- and long-term memory loss. So, studying for their exams and keeping up with their peers gets harder. That's how a straight-A-student ends up scoring Ds and worse, much to the shock of their parents, who cannot seem to understand this change.

- **Their mental health suffers:** Drugs can impair the brain or central nervous system, leading to learning difficulties and paving the way for serious mental disorders.

- **They become reckless:** With drugs coursing through their bodies, teens who abuse drugs often behave in a way that puts their lives at risk. They drive fast, chase adrenaline through dangerous activities, or engage in other harmful activities. It puts them at risk of injury or even death.

Drugs may look like fun, but their effects are not. But most teens don't know that–they only know what they see in movies or social media. Or the *high* they feel when they've smoked a blunt or chugged some beers. To them, it might all look like fun and games. So, how do you help them realize drugs are not all that?

How to Talk to Your Teen About Drugs

He became very good at disguising his drug habit. Throughout high school, he excelled on the baseball team and was the third-highest scorer on the lacrosse team. He insisted he was okay, but he really wasn't.

You would think that '*the birds and the bees*' was the hardest conversation I ever held with my teen. But it wasn't–it was the drugs talk. It was the day I drew in a sharp breath and started talking to my son about why doing drugs was not cool. It was when I realized just how much danger revolved around my precious child–and how little control I had over what happened to him. The fear that went through me and the emotions welling up inside me said it all–I was scared. But I had to push through my feelings and do what was right for him–to educate him rather than scare him. I had seen what scaring teens did, and I did not want my son thinking that I was not a safe space. So, how did I handle this scary talk? What can you do to get through to your child?

- **Open those communication channels:** Chapter five is at it again. And it makes sense because *talking at* your child has never worked. These young minds craving independence want a seat at the table, so give it to them. I know how hard it is to relinquish control, especially when you think you are protecting your child. But that can push them to rebel rather than listen to you. So, instead, open those doors by clarifying that you want to talk rather than dictate. Here are some conversation starters you could use:

- Drug use has reduced in the last ten years. Do you think those statistics are accurate?
- There's a debate on the safety of marijuana use. What do you feel about this?

Allow your teen to give their point of view. And even if you feel they are wrong, don't interject or shush them. Listen, and when it's your turn, you can offer your two cents.

- **Point out where you stand:** Like with sex, every family has a stance on some of these crucial issues. So, where do you stand on drugs? Let your teen know. For example, you might be okay with *your teen sipping on wine when they are eighteen.* Or you might be the parent that feels that *you would prefer that your teen never uses drugs.* Explain why you feel the way you do so your teen can understand your reasoning. You can also explore the risks of drugs, ensuring that you are objective in doing so. For example, *impaired thinking* is a reasonable risk. Try to figure out the facts and not pass on myths to your kid. Otherwise, they will start believing what other sources say when they find gaps in your explanations. And it will not always be helpful.

Also, be clear. Some parents use such ambiguous language that it paves the way for miscommunication. Here's an example. You could tell your teen to *make the right choice for drugs.* To you, this might mean not abusing drugs. But your teen can interpret this as *using just enough drugs to ensure they don't go over the limit.* Both of you would think you have communicated, but you haven't. And if you ever found your teen using drugs, they would wonder why you were angry about it. Effective communication relies on clarity, so ensure you are direct about where you stand.

- **Ask if your teen has used drugs:** We would all like to assume that our kids have no idea what drugs are–that they have never used drugs. Wouldn't that be great? But it's not always the case. Your child may have experienced a *high* at some point in their life. They could even use drugs now. So, find out if they have been down this path, ask what prompted them to do so. Here are some answers you could expect:

- Someone offered me a pill, and I took it,
- I was curious, so I did it,

- The pressure was getting to me, and this was a way out.

By understanding *why your teen used drugs*, you can discuss their underlying reasons. Say, for example, that your teen says they felt good after taking the drug. Then you can ask them about what's been happening in their life. They might suffer and have no way of dealing with it. Then you can explore healthy ways to get this *feel-good* without resorting to drugs.

But of course, these conversations are not always that easy. Your teen could simply say that they do not want to talk about it. Here, you can encourage them to speak to a trusted adult or professional counselor.

- **Assess your environment:** I knew genetic vulnerabilities existed but did not realize just how strong they were until I witnessed them. One of my friends grew up without ever meeting his father–he knew nothing about the man. Towards his teen years, he started abusing alcohol. By the time he was twenty, his drinking had taken a dangerous turn. In his twenties, we learned his dad had also suffered alcoholism. These two men who had never laid an eye on each other had somehow suffered the fate of genes. So, you consider your child may be genetically predisposed to drug abuse. Is that the case? Does anyone in your family suffer from substance abuse? Then this might be the time to be open about this with your child. If they understand they are at more risk than others, they can exercise better judgment in their decisions. Most of my friend's family knew about his father's past, but none shared it with him. So, even as he found himself lost in drinking, he did not know why it was happening. And I can't help but feel that it must have been a very traumatizing experience for him.

- **Offer an olive branch:** We cannot forget that teens are impulsive and could make the wrong decisions even when they had intended otherwise. So, your child could go to a party, smoke marijuana, realize what they've done, and feel scared of coming home. What then? Should they drive in that condition, or should they come to you for help? Clarify that you will be there for them if they need you–that they don't need to put themselves at risk if they ever take drugs. Once they get home safely, you can let them sleep it off, and you can talk about it the next day.

- **Keep the conversation going:** Like with the *birds and the bees*, you need to keep talking to your teen about drugs. Keep in mind that many factors can trigger your teen to develop substance abuse. So, while anxiety might be the major risk now, added pressure next year could push them closer to the edge. As the circumstances in their life changes, so will the likelihood of abusing drugs. And checking in can help you keep tabs on their state of mind as this happens.

I know that this conversation is difficult, but it can shed light on your teen's stance on drugs. It also enables you to impart your family values to your child. As you do so, you might realize that your child is further down the road than you expected. Then, in this case, you would be better off liaising with a professional counselor to help you navigate this delicate situation.

Is Your Teen on Drugs?

In his senior year of high school, his car was firebombed in the driveway of our home. In retrospect, we realized it was drug-related, but the explanation he gave us made sense. It was all a lie.

Even with open communication channels, your child might still not be forthcoming about their drug abuse. They might admit to using drugs in the past, but will probably not tell you they have a stash in their room. Or that they get high just to get through school. Why?–because drug abuse often paves the way for deception. Teens learn that to keep up with the drug use, they must lie–about how they use their money, where they spend their time, why they are suddenly getting in accidents, etc. So, lying to you about not being on drugs will be just another lie on top of the many they've told in the past.

And while it would be nice to take your child's word for it, you cannot afford to rely on this alone. Instead, you must keep an eye out for the following signs of drug abuse:

- **Their personality has changed:** We earlier covered that mood changes may result from mental disorders like anxiety and depression. But sometimes, it comes down to drug abuse. Teens on drugs often exhibit:
  - Signs of withdrawal or depression,
  - A sudden lack of motivation,
  - Unwillingness to communicate with you or other people in the household,
  - Silence, hostility, or even anger,
  - A need to keep things secret from you, coupled with an increase in deception. A child who used to

divulge every bit of their day now suddenly seems vested in keeping to themselves,
- A lack of focus,
- Increased impulsivity and
- An unexplained increase in activity. They seem highly active and experience bursts of energy that you cannot seem to pin down.

- **Their behavior is now questionable**: You often realize that your teen is now coming into their own–you can see it in the way they carry themselves. Most of these instances should not be hair-rising. But when your teen shows the signs below, it might be time to pay more attention to why they are acting differently:
  - Their interactions with their peers and family have changed.
  - They no longer seem interested in their hobbies and show less interest in school, work, or other activities. They may even miss school.
  - They cannot look you in the eye and attempt to avoid one-on-one conversations.
  - They want to keep to themselves more, including locking their doors and disappearing for unexplained periods.

- They no longer respect the boundaries in place and often go out and come back way after the curfew.
- They do not want anyone looking over their shoulders when using their phones or gadgets.
- They seem to have a ton of excuses to justify their behavior, so whenever you question their actions, they come up with a reason on the spot. And something tells you that these excuses are made up.
- They often use mints or gum to hide their breath. So, even if you get a whiff of smoke, you get this overpowering minty breath that confuses your nostrils, or they use a lot of perfume or cologne to mask any smoke on their person.
- They seem to be always out of cash, and you have noticed that they are running through their savings or pocket money fast. If you have access to their account, you can tell that they are suddenly spending money and can't tell you where they have directed it.
- They have resorted to stealing from you or selling their possessions, and you cannot understand why they need this extra cash.

- They are now walking into things or stumbling all over the place. It's almost as if they have poor coordination and balance.
- Their energy levels fluctuate a lot. One minute, they are highly active, and the next, they need to sleep it off.

- **Their appearance has changed**: You can't help but notice that something feels off. It could be because:

- They no longer pay much attention to their hygiene–their room looks a mess; they dress as if they don't care about what they look like and seem to have let go of basic hygiene rules like brushing and bathing.
- They often come home smelling of smoke or other smells that you cannot quite place.
- They show physical signs of using drugs: burn marks on lips and fingers, track marks on their legs or arms, flushed cheeks, shaking, constantly dry lips, etc. And to hide this, they may start wearing long sleeves or using makeup on their body.

- **Their health has suffered:** We all know that drugs put our bodies at a disadvantage. But does this show in our physical state? Well, yes! A teen who is on drugs will:

- Often fall sick: Their immune system seems to lose more fights than it wins. They perspire a lot, suffer seizures, often vomit, etc. So, you find you need to have medicines around or take them to the hospital often.
- Show signs of a poor health state: Examples include allergies, sores, spots in and around the mouth, bruising on the skin, eye redness, etc. And you cannot seem to pin these signs down to any sickness or allergies.
- Gain or add weight dramatically, yet there is no underlying eating disorder.
- Complain of feeling tired despite getting enough hours of sleep.

- **They are leaving evidence around the home**: As much as your teen will try to cover up any traces of drug use, they might still leave some crumbs for you to find. These include:
  - Containers or wrappers you cannot recognize and don't know the contents of,
  - Drug-related devices like syringes, eye drops, smoking devices, lighters, etc.

- Dents in your car that you know you did not cause. You know you left the car in the garage in good condition, and yet it now seems to have been in an accident. And when you ask about such changes, your teen appears to be as clueless as you are.

- Drugs going missing: You notice that your medicine cabinet is short of pills, or your beer cans have reduced, etc.

Does your child exhibit any of these signs and symptoms? Please note that some of these changes might just be part of your teen's transition into adulthood. For example, they may be moody because of hormones. Or they might dress poorly because they *no longer care that much about their appearance.* Drugs are not the sole cause of such changes.

So, you will need to do a bit more digging. How?

- **Sniff them:** When your child comes home, smell them, and see if they smell like they have been smoking or drinking,

- **Look them in the eye:** Do their eyes seem red? Are their eyelids uncharacteristically heavy? Look for any signs that they might be on drugs.

- **Observe them:** Do they come home stumbling all over the place? Or elated for no reason? Do they appear withdrawn or tired after a night out? If they behave differently after being out of the house, this could point to drug use.

- **Investigate:** We all dread when we invade our teens' spaces, searching for the truth. But if the need arises, we must step up to the plate. And this is one of those instances. So, check under their bed, in drawers, in small boxes, between books, under the floorboards, in their closets, pretty much everywhere.

If none of these checks point to drug use, then your teen might battle a mental struggle. And it might be time to investigate that. However, if you think there is more to this sudden change in demeanor, it might be time to work with a professional who can point you in the right direction. Is there anything else you can do if the assessment proves that your child is doing drugs? Yes, please refer to the next section for some pointers.

How to Help Your Teen Quit Drugs

He shared some things from his heart with me the summer before he died, and I developed some insight into the private pain he had held onto for so long. He had so much regret over his drug use.

Are you equipped to help your teen stop using drugs? That's a question that most people grapple with on learning that their children are actively using drugs. I will start by stating that it's a journey I would not wish on any parent– an experience that will be as hard on you as it will be on your child. I have seen first-hand how hard it can be to get a teen off drugs. And I know it can get messy. But with professional help on your side, a lot of patience, understanding, unlearning, and learning, I know you can do it. I believe you are the key to getting your kid on the other side of this. And here's how you can do it:

- **Take a deep breath:** I can imagine you going through your teen's closet and finding a can of beer or a marijuana blunt. And I know that the emotions that would follow can be pretty varied–anger, concern, fear, hurt, disappointment, etc. Do you know what experts agree on doing at this point? Now is the time to calm down rather than marching up to your child with their stash in tow. Remove yourself from the situation, take a walk, call someone, and don't do it no matter how tempted you are to talk about what you have seen.

Process your emotions, allow yourself to feel, and just be in the moment.

- **Get the facts:** Once you have collected your thoughts, talk to a doctor, and know the risks associated with the said drug. What does it do? How addictive is it? Understand the working of the drug so that as you talk to your teen, they can see that you are coming from a knowledgeable point of view. Else, you can start talking about *alcohol* like it's a *hard drug,* and this tone will derail the conversation. They will feel you are attacking them rather than communicating with them.

- **Open the communication door:** We talked earlier about how you can talk to your teen about drugs. Now that it's clear that they have used drugs, they can open up about where they got the drugs and why they used them. Are they struggling in school? How do they feel? Is there anything that's pushing them to use? Ask questions and **listen** to your child.

- **Be supportive:** It's easy to feel like now is the time to firmly stamp your authority in the household. But now, your child needs to know that you still care about them. Be firm but still show them the love they need–clarify that you are there for them, and they can come to you with questions or for help.

- **Don't be an enabler:** Sometimes, parents of teens could enable their behavior without even knowing that they are doing so. How? *By ignoring what their teens are doing right under their noses. Or shifting the blame to other people or situations. You could even try to cover up your teen's problem by minimizing it or making light of it when probed by people.* These are just some ways you could avoid the reality of your teen's situation. And you know what this would communicate to your teen?–that it's okay to keep doing drugs.

- **Talk to your teen about the rules:** Now that you appear calm and educated, you can now broach your stance on drugs. Break it down that you will not allow them to use any drugs, regardless of whether it's at home, school, the mall, or any other instance. Be clear and ensure you don't leave any wiggle room they could exploit to abuse drugs. Enforce more boundaries, as we had discussed in earlier chapters. And as you do so, explain the need to have these additional rules. Ensure that your child is part of this process to know the reasoning behind each rule and the consequences that will follow non-compliance. Oh, and you can't waver on these rules because your child's wellbeing is at stake.

- **Get help:** Being there for your teen by yourself can be challenging. So, build a network to help you watch over your teen. Engage your friends, your child's peers, school counselors, other family members, and other people you can trust in this journey. It will make decision-making more manageable and enable you to keep tabs on your child. You cannot do this alone.

- **Keep watching out for signs of drug use:** Even having explained the risks of doing drugs and laid out the rules, your teen could continue using drugs. So, you need to monitor them. Are they showing any signs of drug use? If yes, you might need to get professional help.

- **Engage a professional:** Unless you are a professional, you are not equipped to gauge if your teen is addicted or just experimenting with drugs. So, please don't make this decision without having your child assessed by someone with the know-how to center on what's troubling them. Else, you could try to get your kid off hard drugs with rules and love, which is hardly enough.

- **Get your teen into counseling:** Some teens do better in support groups, others prefer counseling, and others make do with talking to someone they trust. Once you understand what's pushing your teen to do drugs, you will need to create an environment to deal with the underlying causes. Otherwise, they will still feel inclined to abuse drugs, despite knowing the risks.

Remember to respond with affection and show your child that you still care about them despite using drugs. Second, do not blame yourself for what's happening–there's a lot that could drive your child to drugs. So, even with open communication and providing them with a safe space, they could still decide to experiment with drugs. Rather than focus on what's gone wrong, be proactive and look into what you can do. And don't forget to ask for help.

Is it Time for Rehab?

"Mom, I messed up. It is not Dad's fault, Larry (his stepfather), or your fault. I take responsibility. I messed up." My heart was broken. But he couldn't stop using drugs.

To admit or not to admit your child?–That's another challenging consideration you will face with your teen. Rehab is not always easy–and I am not even talking about the stigma associated with it. I am talking about how hard it is to get a teen to accept to go into rehab. Most people don't want to admit that they have a problem, and even when they go to rehab, they don't commit to it. And when they come out, some fall into the traps of drug abuse because they don't accept that they cannot handle the effects of the drugs. They think they have what it takes to get high and remain in control. That's why rehab is always more effective when your teen feels they need it.

But does that mean you should watch them waste away as they hold on to the belief that all is swell? Not at all. The longer your teen abuses drugs, the harder it will be for them to kick the habit. If the professional assessment points to addiction that requires rehabilitation, you have no choice but to admit your child. Mild abuse often requires outpatient treatment where your child does not have to leave home for days at a time. They go in, get counseling, and still live under your roof, bathing in the comfort of familiarity. Of course, most of us would prefer such an option.

But when dealing with opioid addictions and other hard drugs, the professional assessment could reveal that your child is better off with inpatient treatment. It is imperative when dealing with substance use disorders. So, which way forward to your family? Well, that's a decision best arrived at with a professional on your team. To get better results, ensure that your teen is part of the process because they will be more willing to accept the treatment that way.

You might have noticed that this chapter is quite lengthy. And it is for a good reason–drugs destroy lives, not just of the teens but the family overall. Watching a loved one waste away due to drug use or addiction is heartbreaking. And if we can save our teens in the nick of time, we can stand a better chance against this drug epidemic. My thoughts and well wishes go out to you.

***

Chapter Fifteen

Teen Pregnancies: What To Do When The Stork Pays Your Teen A Visit

"Pregnancy and birth are significant contributors to high school dropout rates among girls. Only about fifty percent of teen mothers receive a high school diploma by twenty-two years of age, whereas approximately ninety percent of women who do not give birth during adolescence graduate from high school." –CDC

*A*nne was only eighteen, bright-eyed and always ready with a smile. She oozed so much life that it *was almost impossible to process all that she had been through. This young lady toiled in the neighborhood store as a clerk by day, and at night, she would babysit for families. She barely had time to go out like her friends or just take the day off and sit at home catching up on social media. Unlike most people her age, she had two mouths to feed. At only eighteen, she was raising twin boys aged two. And I could not help but wonder how this was. So, I probed delicately, concerned about this young girl who was my son's age at the time.*

How Teens Get Pregnant

You might wonder why I wanted to know how Anne ended up as a teen parent. In my years, I have realized that teen parents are often termed as immoral, selfish, and have many other negative connotations. People think they wished the pregnancy upon themselves–that they willingly had unprotected sex, aware of the consequences and uncaring about what that would spell in their lives. Sure, I know teens who got pregnant just to get emancipated. But in most cases, you find a teen gets pregnant because:

- **They are under the influence of drugs or alcohol.** We covered in the previous chapter that drugs impair one's thinking. At what point in a drunken stupor do you stop and think that *you should wear a condom* to avoid getting pregnant? You don't–so you go all the way, and a few weeks later, hell breaks loose. And most teens don't even realize just how bad their thinking can get when they are *high.*

- **They do not have any positive influences**. It's easy to imagine that every child has caring parents and grows up in a society that embraces them. But is that always the case? Not at all. Some kids grow up being told that they will not amount to anything–that their parents expect little of them. Some grow up in societies with low educational successes and don't think there is much to live for. And their peers have the same thinking. So, when one thing leads to the other, and they fall pregnant or impregnate someone, they don't think of it as a life-changing event. It's just one of the many negative experiences in their lives.

- **They do not understand safe sex**. I discussed the need to be open about sex. Why? While we are not exactly handing condoms to our kids and going *"have fun,"* we must protect them from unsafe sex. Pregnancy is not the only adverse consequence of unprotected sex–we also must think about STIs. But for most kids? The *birds and* *the bees* talk is a foreign concept. They grow up sheltered from the truth and understand that sex is taboo. So, when they eventually have sex, they have no way to protect themselves–nobody to take them through wearing condoms or how to get an emergency pill. They are on their own, which is just a recipe for disaster.

- **They give in to peer pressure.** We have also covered why peer pressure could push your kid into experimenting with harmful activities. And sex is not so far down that list. You probably remember what it was like in high school–it seemed like everyone was having sex. And the virgins? Some people would resort to taunting them just to inch them closer to having sex. And while we would like to think that kids would be immune to such pressure, we all know that it's not always the case.

- **They are sexually abused.** How often do people talk about the teens who fell pregnant owing to sexual abuse? *Those who were raped? Those who were in violent relationships where consent was not a factor? Teens who dated adults who took advantage of them? Children whose relatives turned on them and forced or encouraged them to have sex with them?* Who talks about these cases and their prevalence in society? As a result, some kids fall pregnant even when they do all they can to avoid it.

- **They idealize teen pregnancies.** Have you paid attention to the number of shows that make teen pregnancies look cool? Take *Teen Mom* as an example. It makes the whole experience look fun, and a teenager watching the show and seeing just how famous the teen moms are could think it's a good choice. They know nothing about the sleepless nights with a newborn, the endless calls to the doctor when a child has colic, or just how expensive babies are. All they see are teens who get to decide about their lives, almost as if they are adults. And some can get pregnant, thinking that it's all fun and games.

While these are the main reasons, your teen could fall pregnant or impregnate someone for a wildly different reason. For example, they might have felt depressed and thought a baby was on the way out. I heard this one too–the girl in question felt so lonely and thought that if she had a baby in her life, she would have something to live for–how heartbreaking.

Oh, and I must point out that this chapter may lie more on the teen girl side. After all, while it is pretty unfair, girls endure the pregnancies. They are the ones who put a hold on school, the ones who nurse the babies, and the ones who do most of the heavy lifting. They are the most affected. And I know just how unfair that may seem–that the boy gets to live his life almost as if it never happened. I could go on about the tragedy of this situation, but that would not help matters. We can't dwell on what we cannot fix. Instead, we must think about how we can help our girls if they fall pregnant–and how we can also hold the boys accountable for their part in it. Most importantly, the role we can play as parents.

The Declining Cases of Teenage Pregnancies

"The national teen pregnancy rates for ages fifteen to seventeen and eighteen to nineteen (the number of pregnancies per 1,000 females in the specified age group) have declined almost continuously for nearly thirty years. The decline has been most striking among teens ages fifteen to seventeen by eighty-two percent, from 74.8 pregnancies per 1,000 females ages fifteen to seventeen in 1989 to 13.6 in 2017." – **CDC**

Anne was like most other teens–excited about life and eager to see what lay ahead in her journey. She'd grown up in a friendly neighborhood with strict parents who watched her every move. They had a plan for her–she would be an accountant, just like them. But their plan did not pan out as expected. A cute boy moved in next door along the road, and despite her parents' strictness, Anne sneaked a few visits to see this boy. A few weeks later, she fell sick, and her mother shipped her off to her aunt's place, unable to deal with what she termed as the shame that Anne had brought into the family.

How Teen Pregnancies Affect Teens

Shame–what a way to describe a teen pregnancy. But that's what many parents think about when their teens fall pregnant or impregnate others. They think of how badly this will affect their lives–their pedestals in society. But what of the teen? Studies have proven that teen parents and their children often have a pretty rough adjustment in this world. They grapple with:

- **High Dropout Rates:** Most teen moms must leave school for a considerable while during their third trimester. Others even leave before starting their second trimester. And unfortunately, once the baby is born, most teens are left to raise the babies and cater to their financial needs. The result?–they must quit school and start working. Most of them find themselves thrust into the workforce, forced to take up casual jobs to make ends meet. And eventually, those are the only positions available to them because they never get to go back to school. Most of them never get that diploma, let alone pursue a college education.

- **Low economic status:** We know how competitive the job market is. Even with an undergraduate degree, you are at a disadvantage. Imagine not having a high school diploma–you'd be forced to take up the jobs that other people do not want. And for most teen parents, this is the reality. They can't negotiate on better terms because they don't have the qualifications. Earning the base rates in industries despite working long hours pushes them closer and closer to poor living conditions. Most of them rely on government and donor aids just to make it through each month.

- **Becoming adults overnight:** We have already covered that adolescents deal with the sudden onset of adulthood. They are not children, but they are not adults either. And this balancing act is not an easy one. But most teens have the time to figure out what adults they want to be. Teen parents figure it out within months. One minute, they are like other teens, wondering who the next social media guru will be. And the next? They are counting change just to see if it's enough to buy diapers for the week. This sudden emotional, psychological, and physical transition is not easy. And if they were already dealing with mental distress, it could become worse.

- **A change in peer groups:** What happens to teens who get pregnant? Diapers and playgroups are not exactly the conversations that teens wish to hold. So, a teen parent has it hard fitting in with other teens. While others post about new gadgets and crazy social media challenges, teen parents follow childcare and baby essentials pages. They realize just how isolated they are from their peers in weeks or months. And that can make them feel lost on top of all the other emotions coursing through their bodies.

- **Poor health habits:** What were you eating as a teen? I remember that I often snacked on junk food between meals and would have preferred pizza and soda over any veggies. Unfortunately, that's what most teens eat. And even when pregnant, they deem unhealthy food as okay.

Some don't even have access to junk food because they get put out by their parents. So, coming across malnourished teen parents is relatively easy. And unfortunately, this affects the baby in utero and the mother.

- **A loss of identity:** Teen parents go from being teens to being parents overnight. They go from being high school students to being responsible for a whole other being. And that can be overwhelming, especially when they have no emotional and psychological support.

The whole teen parenting experience can be too much for a teen to bear. And it's not uncommon for teens to feel depressed, battling alienation and a sudden increase in societal pressures. Coming across teen parents who have succumbed to suicide breaks my heart. But it's not hard to see how one could end up in those shoes. That's why we must be there for our kids.

Why Teen Pregnancies Are on The Decline

Teen pregnancies were quite common in the 70s and 80s. Even as I wrote this book, I thought the rates were still high– what with the horror stories I kept hearing from my peers. Somehow, it seemed like everyone believed our kids were doomed to become parents at an early age. My neighbors and friends were freaking out about the possibilities. And who could blame them? One of my neighbors had realized that her son, aged thirteen, was already having sex. And how did she chance upon this discovery? Well, she found condom wrappers under his bed–which he claimed to have picked up on a bus. Quite the story! So, I could see why she and many other parents were scared that their kids could become parents. But amid this fear, I realized that the teen pregnancy rates had *actually* reduced. We are now recording historic lows. To give you a visual, the rates have dropped by an average of fifty percent since the 90s. Most pregnancies occur at ages eighteen to nineteen, which is quite an improvement. But why have the rates gone down? (Not that I am complaining)

It's not that kids are not having sex. Kids are having sex at much earlier ages. The reason behind this decline is the improved efficacy and use of contraception. By the time most kids are sixteen, they know precisely what condoms do, and some are even on the pill. So, as much as they might be sexually active, their chances of getting pregnant or impregnating someone are considerably low. That's what research points to, and I believe it. To what can we credit for this increased use of contraception?

- Parents are more willing to talk to their kids about sex,
- More sex education programs are being launched in schools, and
- Increased access to sex education–teens can learn to protect themselves online. Thus, a teen who does not have adequate support at home and in school can find peers or trusted sites to learn how to be careful.

As a result, kids are now delaying sexual experiences, understanding the risks of being sexually active. And those who are having sex are now careful about the number of partners they have and are actively using contraceptives. But, do you want to know the interesting thing about most of the research I encountered when studying teen pregnancies?–preaching abstinence does not work. Kids want the truth–they want us to acknowledge what sex is rather than bury our heads in the sand. They want us to teach them how to be safe. Telling them to wait until marriage or until they are in college only pushes them closer to the deed. So, abstinence programs have mainly proven ineffective at delaying or even preventing teen sexual experiences.

Taylor DeBruce

What To Do When Your Teenager is Going to be a Parent

"The children of teenage mothers are more likely to have lower school achievement and to drop out of high school, have more health problems, be incarcerated during adolescence, give birth as a teenager, and face unemployment as a young adult."
–CDC

Cast out and living with her aunt she had met once or twice during her formative years, Anne felt isolated. Her boyfriend had no means of reaching her, and her parents would hear none of the talks about relocating her to the city. A few months into her pregnancy, Anne would not only give birth to one, but two children. Upon that revelation, her aunt's tune changed–she did not want to be responsible for two newborns. And she clarified it was time for Anne to head back to her parents' home.

Anne's mother was probably pale from the news–nobody prepares you to deal with teen pregnancy. As a parent, I would not wish such an experience on any teen. I remember how heavy I was with my son, unable to work, study, or even sleep. For those months that I carried him in

330

my womb, my body belonged to him. I even left work and quit my evening classes three months before the delivery. By the time they wheeled me out of that hospital, I was sure I didn't want to relive the whole pregnancy experience. But it was not just about dedicating my body to another being– it was also the emotional and psychological strain. I didn't even know that pregnancy brain was a thing until I realized just how bad my reasoning had become, even after giving birth. Pregnancies are pretty different, and my friends have shared their stories with me. Some went into postpartum depression (before doctors even recognized it existed), others had to undergo last-minute surgeries, others felt alienated from their bodies, and others just felt off.

Of course, there are great pregnancy stories. But you know that when you have been through a weird experience, your mind somehow goes to the worst plausible scenarios. So, to hear that your child is pregnant, you would probably be at a loss of where to start. Let's try to make this experience easier:

Assess what you are feeling

I cannot even imagine what you might have felt at this point. Is it shock? How about embarrassment? Are you disappointed with your child? Is worrying about your child's future crippling you? Or maybe it's guilt, and you feel you did not do enough to protect them. It's a joy for some parents because their teens are mature and can handle the additional responsibility.

Whatever you are feeling is normal–you have a right to feel the way you do. Besides, nobody could have prepared you for this. Take some time to assess your emotions, and instead of acting on them, calm down. Reflect on what this means for your teen–keep in mind that their emotional wellbeing boils down to the baby. And if they have a strong support system, they can likely have a healthy pregnancy.

If you cannot bring yourself to accept what's happening or need more help, seek counseling. Talking to a therapist can help you sort out your feelings, so you do not project them onto your vulnerable teen.

Walk In Your Teen's Shoes

In an earlier chapter, we had talked about the need to understand what our children are going through. Now, more than ever, you must seek to understand them. Your teen was probably not thinking about changing diapers and enrolling their baby in daycare. Instead, they cared about their social media presence, peers, fashion, tech, etc. But now, they are grappling with this extra responsibility, scared, ashamed, and probably in denial. Your teen probably thinks you are angry and disappointed with them (which is likely accurate). But beating themselves up about it only contributes to mental distress. Even teen boys go through a lot when they realize that they have impregnated someone -they are often not ready to be fathers. So, they do not know how to step in and may feel inclined to escape this new responsibility.

Communicate

Your teen cannot know what you think if you do not express it. And the same goes for them–you cannot tell what they feel unless you ask them. Once you have calmed down and processed your emotions, sit your teen down and explain the reality of parenthood to them. Let them know the hard truths–that her life will change, and she'll be wholly responsible for this new life she has created.–That she will need to grow up faster than her peers and that it's not always going to be rosy. Clarify that you will be there to help her and discuss:

- **Does your teen want to keep the baby?** Your teen could be inclined to keep the baby, give it up for adoption, or terminate the pregnancy. Which way does she want to go? Keep in mind that this decision affects your teen's life. So, while you may want to weigh in on what direction she chooses, allow her to take over the reins. You are welcome to offer advice, and you can also engage professionals to give their input. A therapist, a GP, and a trusted friend could help you with this.

- **Is the baby's father going to be involved in raising the baby?** I mentioned earlier that boys continue with their lives almost as if nothing happened. Is this the case with your teen's partner? Are they interested in helping her raise the baby? Often, parents think that marrying the teens off is a good idea–setting them up to start a family. But you should not push such notions on your teen unless they are open to it. Consider that your teen is probably not in the best state to make such pertinent decisions. Instead of rushing to such decisions, work out a plan with the teen boy and his parents. They can decide just how involved they want to be, and you can agree on the way forward. If marriage is on the table, hold off on the talks until the baby is home.

PS: Do not blame the father for the pregnancy–he was not alone in this decision. Doing so will only alienate him from your daughter, who needs his support. However, if the pregnancy was not a result of consensual sex, that amounts to rape. So, get the authorities involved and ensure you loop your daughter in on this.

- **Does your teen want to keep going to school?** Some teens are okay with pushing on in school until the last trimester. Others feel so self-conscious that they cannot keep going. Encourage your teen to stay in school for as long as they can. And even if they decide to quit until they deliver the baby, let them know you are open to them resuming school once the baby is home. That way, your teen does not pump the brakes on her education and career. Of course, it's okay if she wants to stay home during the pregnancy–she'll probably need this time to adjust to her new role.

- **Does your teen want you involved in the pregnancy?** We often assume that our kids want us to be part of the journey. But is this the case? How involved does your daughter want you to be? Perhaps she's already working and feels she can cater to her baby financially. Or she wants you to provide for the baby in all aspects. Maybe she even wants you to adopt the baby and raise it as your own. So, instead of assuming what your teen wants, ask her.

- **How much support are you willing to give your teen?** Raising a child requires a lot — emotionally, financially, psychologically. And the more support that a teen has, the better equipped they are as parents. So, how much are you willing to step in? Are there areas you feel your teen must cater to? Say, for example, you want them to work a part-time job and go to school once the baby is home. That way, they can contribute to some expenses.

- **Who will pay for the pregnancy-related expenses?** Pregnant teens need a lot. So, who's paying for the doctor's visits? How about the clothes and food? Now is the time to discuss this.

- **Where will your daughter live?** Will she live with you? How about when the baby is born? It might look like a weird discussion, but it matters. Once the baby is home and crying all night, you'll be happy that you weighed in on this decision. It's better than feeling resentful that you are held back and are now swamped with a new responsibility.

- **Will you look after your grandchild when your daughter is at school or at work?** Your teen will need someone to help them out when they are away. Will this be you, or will your teen need to hire someone? If it's you, just how available will you be?

If some of these discussions seem awkward or you cannot agree on one thing, engage a therapist. Then you can be objective about what you want and avoid arguing with each other where possible.

Seek Medical Care

Pregnant teens need medical care from an early stage in their pregnancy. While most teen girls can handle the pregnancy to maturity, they are still at high risk of complications. Therefore, get your teen medical attention the minute you realize they are pregnant to avoid such occurrences. Doctors screen teens for any STDs and assess their overall health to prepare for the baby. They can then advise you, the teen, and other caregivers on:

- **The medical care required during the pregnancy:** That should include the number of prenatal visits and how to deal with common pregnancy side effects,

- **The changes** she will experience emotionally and physically,

- **The supplements the teen will need** to promote a healthy pregnancy–folic acid, iron, calcium, and others as deemed necessary by the doctor,

- **The substances your teen must limit or avoid during pregnancy:** These include smoking, alcohol, drugs, caffeine, etc. If your teen is on drugs, the doctor will suggest ways to help her quit,

- How much **sleep** your teen should get,

- **The risks** associated with unsafe sex during pregnancy,

- **The best nutrition concerning her current health status:** Includes proteins, enough calcium, adequate iron, and folic acid. Also, your teen cannot go on a diet during pregnancy as it can harm her and the baby. If you notice any signs of an eating disorder, please discuss this with her GP,

- **How much exercise your teen should get:** Your teen could try to counter the pregnancy weight gain with hardcore workouts. Working out is okay if your teen is already fit and engages in safe activities for her and the baby. Besides, it also makes the labor easier and the pregnancy easier to carry. However, too much working out can be detrimental to her health and baby.

- **How to manage stress:** Your teen will probably process various emotions. From anger to resentment to disappointment, your teen could struggle mentally. And if this is not addressed, she could direct these negative emotions to her baby. Talk to your teen's doctor about how you can help your teen manage pregnancy-related stress. She will need even more help when the baby is home.

Enroll Her In Prenatal Classes

What better way to prepare for being a parent than taking a class? These classes cater not only to birthing. Instead, they also delve into basics like feeding, child safety, diapering, etc. It's best to enroll your teen in a teen-specific class where they can meet other pregnant teens. This community can boost their mental health and feel more comfortable with this new responsibility.

Be Supportive

So, your teen daughter is pregnant, and your worst nightmare might have come true. And deep down, you might wish that you could turn back the clock and get her on the pill just in time. But that's not the case. So, instead of expecting the baby away, it's time to embrace your teen. Listen to her concerns and fears, and address each one as they come along. There will be times when she will need you more than others–be there. And as she learns to be a good parent, so will you, which could be one of the most rewarding experiences of your life.

Also, even as cravings hit your daughter hard, encourage her to make healthy choices. Make healthy meals at home, take her on walks, get her counseling, and do what it takes to help her care for herself. Don't forget to practice self-care, too, and do not neglect your own needs. Yes, your daughter needs you, but you also need to care for yourself.

Talk to Your Other Kids

Studies show that siblings to teen parents are likely to become teen parents too. So, now is the time to talk to your other children about the risks of unsafe sex. Do not demonize your pregnant teen. This talk is just to educate your other kids and protect them from this parental responsibility.

So, what happens if your teen terminates the pregnancy or gives her baby up for adoption? That's hard because the emotional responses associated with these decisions are quite varied. I've known people who gave up their babies for adoption only to look for them later, haunted by this decision. I've also seen others who terminated their pregnancies and still regret them decades later. So, I would not even want to assume that these decisions are easy for someone, especially a teen. And that's why we need to support our teens–let them know we are there for them from the start. That way, when they eventually decide to terminate a pregnancy or give up their baby, they will do so, knowing that they had other options available–that it was not the only way. Still, instead, it was how they felt *right* to them. And just to ensure that they are comfortable with this decision, please involve a therapist or a trusted counselor. And no matter how inclined you feel to stomp your foot on the ground-based on your values, remember that this decision is not yours to make. So, make your peace with that, and be the shoulder to lean on that they direly need.

Parenting the Soon-to-be Parent

"The declines in national teen pregnancy rates have been reflected in declines in birth rates and abortion rates. In 2017, the majority — about fifty-eight percent — of pregnancies to adolescent females ages fifteen to seventeen ended in birth, and twenty-eight percent ended in abortion; for teens ages eighteen to nineteen, sixty-two percent of pregnancies ended in birth, and twenty-three percent ended in an abortion." –CDC

Anne's mother was very clear about her stance–give the children up for adoption, go back to school, and act as if it had never happened. Besides, very few people knew Anne was pregnant. The minute she'd fallen sick and tested positive for pregnancy, her mother had swiftly moved her out of the home. So, if she did not have the evidence (twins) to boot when she came back home, her parents could still face their neighbors with a straight face. But this solution did not bode well for Anne, and she refused to give up her kids.

So, as a parent, does your role change when your teen falls pregnant or impregnates someone? Do they suddenly become independent and free to make their decisions? Do they still need to listen to what you have to say? Well, first, you acknowledge that they've been thrust into adulthood at a young age. Their prefrontal cortex does not develop overnight just because they are becoming parents. They are still impulsive and at the mercy of their emotions. They still need you to guide them on what's right–how to deal with societal pressures, body image issues, eating disorders, and whatnot. You are still a parent and still, need to enforce boundaries like:

- What time can they come home?
- Can they have their partners over at the house?

And when they do not observe the boundaries, take away their privileges like you would have done before - they are still teens even now as they become parents. So, you cannot let them do as they please despite the pushback they may give you. Otherwise, they can take advantage of this and start embarking on activities you had previously banned. So, you need to keep an eye on them and let them know they are still under your roof as much as they are now becoming parents.

You step in as a consultant. You are now talking to another parent who's got a baby to care for, so this is no longer just your child. You now become your child's support system. Let your son or daughter know you care about them, not just by actions, but also by words. Words like *I love you and will support you during this transition. I am here for you, & I can explore the options available to you, which means* a lot to your child. They may already feel judged and unaccepted by others. So, knowing that you are there for them will make a vast difference in their life.

So, it's a balancing act between parenting the teen and embracing the parent they are becoming. Keep the communication lines open so that your child can confide their fears in you. And be ready to listen to them.

What You Can Do to Prepare for the Baby

"The abortion rates for ages fifteen to seventeen and eighteen to nineteen are at their lowest since abortion was legalized in 1973 and are eighty-eight and seventy-nine percent lower than their 1988 peaks, respectively." –CDC

The months went by, slowed by the pressure that was now on this young lady's shoulders. Her mother had cut her off, intent on ridding the family of the shame. She no longer had access to her siblings, and her father was quiet about the issue. On the other side, her aunt had reiterated that Anne had to move out once the twins were born. So, she started working days and doing many odd jobs to raise enough money. A swift surgery later, Anne was a mother to two baby boys. She was only fifteen.

What does a fifteen-year-old know about preparing for a baby?–probably nothing! That's a teen cast into the world, armed with nothing but a pack of diapers and a few essentials. I've been a new mom, and I know just how wild things can become initially. I remember walking around like a zombie, unfeeling and dressed in a loose and dirty shirt, just moving from one room to the other. Despite having a nanny, my sister, and two experienced moms with me, I cried myself to sleep almost every night those first months. I can't even imagine what it's like for a new mom who has no help and no idea what to get before the baby arrives. Can you make this journey easier for your teen? Sure! It starts with early preparations:

- **Encourage your teen to ask questions:** It starts with open communication so your teen can feel comfortable asking you questions. Remember how scary it was to be a first-time parent? That's what your teen is dealing with now.

- **Enroll your teen in a class:** While there is no instruction manual on how to raise a baby, there are basics they should know. For example, how should they feed the baby? How about how to dress a baby without hurting it? They can ask questions you might not have answers to in that class.

- **Get a pediatrician:** It's never too early to vet possible doctors. What hours do they work? How open are they to questions? What are the previous client reviews?

- Prepare the family: The new baby will be part of the family. So, your teen should inform their siblings and other close family members. The sooner others are involved in this process, the easier the transition will be.

- **Set up a space for the baby:** Where will it sleep? Do you have enough room? Select furniture that fits the room to avoid cramping it.

- **Get the essentials:** Babies need a lot of stuff. I'd even forgotten just how much they needed until I paid a visit to my friend in the hospital. So, from diapers to changes of clothes to cribs down to car seats, it's time to shop.

Also, ensure that you disinfect everything you bring home with mild detergents because babies are sensitive.

- **Stock a hospital bag:** You never know when your teen will go into labor, so you must be ready. Fill the bag with personal items, your teen's clothes, documents, diapers, and anything else she will need while in labor.

- **Start babyproofing:** It might seem early to prepare a new child's home. But it's never a good idea to put off safety measures. So, start installing those smoke detectors now.

- **Walk your teen through the changes:** A new mom or dad requires some adjustments. Your teen will likely need to stay away from school and work for the first few months. They will also probably experience some emotional and psychological changes after birth. Educate them on these and advise them to talk to you or a therapist as they anticipate the same.

Ensure that you take on a more advisory role than overseeing the changes. For example, when you go shopping, allow your teen to choose what they like best. Let them choose instead of arguing over whether the wallpaper should be a blue or neutral color. After all, it is still wallpaper, regardless of the hue. And they are the parent!

347

Are You Ready to be a Grandparent?

"In 2011 (the most recent year data available), seventy-five percent of teen pregnancies were unintended (pregnancies that were unwanted entirely or at the time they occurred)." –CDC

The little money she had was what she used to get a place for her children. She only had a few weeks to look for a place to live, with a fresh scar and wailing babies. And in her hand?–she had $500, which was barely enough to cover the necessities. Luckily, one landlord took pity on her, gave her a house, and employed her in his store. That was the start of what was to be a long trudge to caring for her boys.

Can you imagine how hard that must have been? Of course, as parents, we want to do what's best for our kids. So, as a soon-to-be grandparent, what can you do to prepare for your role?

- **Seek therapy:** You cannot be the one guiding your teen on this emotional turmoil if you're not dealing with your emotions. Open up to a therapist, talk to a friend, do whatever it takes to process what you are going through.

- **Let go of the resentment:** Your teen is not the only one who will feel angry about the pregnancy. You could be angry at your child and their baby, and this negativity could cloud your judgment. In the months leading up to the birth of your grandchild, let go of the anger. Take walks, do yoga, meditate, journal, and process it all.

- **Prepare your pockets:** As much as your child may think they've got this responsibility down to an art, they probably do not. For example, where will your fourteen-year-old get enough money to buy diapers and pay for daycare? It's time to line your pockets with some extra cash.

- **Take care of yourself:** Your teen will need enough rest, good food, and adequate hydration during this period. And guess what? So will you! Don't neglect your needs.

- **Allow yourself to grieve:** The dreams you had for yourself and your child are about to change or take a bit of a detour. Feeling sad and hopeless is all part of the deal. Feel it, then release it.

- **Embrace the turn of events:** So, you're about to become a grandparent. Sure, there's the sad aspect to it. But there's also a sea of opportunities tied to the new baby. Think about what could go right and prepare for that.

Your role now is to be a strong support system for your child without neglecting yourself or your other kids. Keep being a reliable partner, a good parent, an available friend, and hold on to the roles you already have. The new baby does not have to put your life on hold, nor does it need to end your teen's. You can all have your cake and eat it.

The Baby's Here! Playing the Grandparent Role

"Not all teen births are first births. In 2019, roughly sixteen percent of live births to fifteen- to nineteen-year-olds were at least the second child born to the mother." –CDC

With no support from her family or baby daddy (who went mute on hearing that there were two surprises on the way), Anne worked day and night. She put a roof over her babies' heads, clothed and fed them. And by the time I met her, she was putting some money together, intent on going back to school for that high school diploma. The confidence in her voice and the radiance in her eyes were proof that she would succeed in this venture. But my heart still broke for this young girl who had faced such a life-changing experience alone–not because she did not have a family, but because they turned their backs on her when she needed them the most. I could not help but wonder what her life would have turned out had they supported her three years ago.

What if they had allowed her to keep schooling?

What if they had not associated her pregnancy with shame?

What if they had helped her care for her babies so she could get her diploma?

What if? What if? What if?

The questions ran through my mind, one after the other. And as I walked away with my shopping bag, I glanced back at Anne, who was now smiling at another customer–there she stood, tall and proud, unknowingly inspiring me to be a more understanding parent.

So, it's been hours of labor, and the doctor comes out of the ward, wipes some sweat off their brow, and goes, "it's a…!" And you breathe a sigh of relief, ask how your daughter is doing, and hug the person closest to you. The baby is here! Now what?

- **Maintain a positive relationship with your teen:** To be a good grandparent, you must be a good parent. Your teen will not embrace your role if they feel you are not supportive of them. So, take a step back and be supportive. And even when you feel left out, do not start imposing your wishes. For example, your daughter might not want you in the labor room. Or your son might not invite you to the baby shower. It's okay–let the new parents do what feels right for them. The less friction they experience from you, the more open they will be towards your role.

- **Maintain a good relationship with the other parents:** Your grandparent will ideally have two sets of grandparents. They could even have more if you are separated from your partner or if the other set of parents has separated. You will meet each other frequently, so it's always good to start on the right foot. Mend any broken fences as you step into your role.

- **Listen to your child:** Each generation raises their kids differently. So, what you use on your child will not appeal to them. Besides, if they listen to what you have to say, what the other parents have to say, what the prenatal class instructor has to say, and so on, they will be lost. Allow the parent(s) to decide what works for them. Oh, and remember the boundaries you'd set for your teen? They will set similar boundaries for you as they raise your grandbaby — respect them.

- **Don't impose your opinions:** It's easy to feel you should teach your teen how to parent. But it appears nagging, especially when you do so, yet your teen has not asked for advice. *So, your teen wants to co-sleep? That's well and good! They don't believe in breastfeeding.–Okay!* If their actions are not harming them or the baby, leave your opinion out of it. Most times, the new parent(s) will try what works out and will not stick to what they are doing now. Butting in will only annoy them and could strain the relationship you are trying to build.

- **Hold off on the shopping:** We already discussed pre-baby shopping. Now that the baby is here, should you splurge on them? It depends on the parent(s). Of course, a few gifts are always welcome. But your teen will probably frown upon you going all out and buying almost everything for them–they want a say in the materials, colors, items, and whatnot. They may even feel like they don't need all that stuff. Perhaps giving them a cheque would be better received and they can put that money into some more important use.

- **Avoid being judgmental:** Your family values might not spill over to your teen's raising techniques. Say, for example, that you believe in circumcision, yet your son does not. That's his choice for his family. All you can do is respect it and, if you have any concerns, voice them respectfully. Or just leave it be.

- **Don't force a relationship:** Step into the grandparent role as soon as the baby is here. But that might not always work–the baby might not bond with you. So, rather than force the wailing child to sit in your arms, just love them from a distance. When they are ready, they will be ready.

- **Do what you are told:** Do just that if your teen asks you to have the baby napping by 2 pm. Respect their rules. Don't start coming up with a new technique, yet they are clear about their wants.

- **Offer help:** new parents need all the help they can get. So, whether it's cooking for them, watching the baby, running errands, or even cleaning up after them, help is always welcome. Sometimes, your teen might not want to ask for help, thinking they can handle it–just jump in and help. Unless they explicitly ask you not to help, be there for them.

Remember that you are not the parent–you are the grandparent. So, it's no longer *whatever you say goes.* Instead, you are there to execute your teen's wishes and offer advice *when asked.* As long as you keep respecting this boundary and the change in roles, you should not clash with your teen. It also sets you up to have a good relationship with your teen and grandbaby.

***

Chapter Sixteen

Supportive Parenting: Being There For Your Teen

"Among teens aged fifteen to sixteen, forty-two percent of teens who don't feel close to their mother and/or father smoke, compared with twenty-six percent of teens who feel close to at least one parent. In this same age group, over thirty-four percent of teens who don't regularly eat dinner with their parents smoked, in contrast to just twenty-five percent of teens who eat dinner regularly with their parents." –Clinton, White House

W hen I was a teen, my parents would force me to eat at the dinner table. It didn't matter how tired I was or how much homework I had waiting for me. Every day at 7 pm without fail, we would switch off the TV and hurdle to the dinner table. Then we would go round, saying what we had done for the day. No matter how mundane the talks became, we gathered, ate together, then left the table to attend to our evening affairs. I thought it was unfair that I could not eat in front of the TV like my neighbors. Why did I have to sit through an hour of "what did you do at school today?" "have you made any new friends?" "have you settled on a college yet?" It all seemed like a waste of time. Sure, we would crack each other up, and we got a glimpse of each other's fears and joys. But all this while, I was inwardly pouting that I could not stuff myself with salad while flipping through a magazine.

Teens aged fifteen to sixteen who do not feel close to their parents are three times more likely to think about suicide than teens close to their parents.

Years later, I understood why this hour each day was so important for our family. I grew fast; boys started noticing me, the homework was piling, and my peer groups were changing. From morning till dusk, I was busy dealing. So, I barely saw my siblings or parents until dinner time. And if they had let me have my way and sit in my room, then I would have been stuck with those thoughts. But at dinner, I got an outlet because there were four ears intent on capturing everything I said. I will not imply that I grew up in a household where we shared everything–not at all. We grew up in an authoritarian household where our parents' word was the law. They took a keen interest in our lives– what we did in school, who we hung out with after school, and so on. I could barely leave the house without giving an itinerary of where I would be and what I would be doing. And even then, I had to get a stamp of approval.

Teens aged fifteen to sixteen who don't eat dinner with their parents regularly are twice as likely to have attempted suicide.

With my parents breathing down my neck, I found myself propelled to do better in everything. I even had to be careful about who I chose as a friend because my parents would vet this individual in all aspects. Eventually, I grew into an all-rounded adult, succeeding in school and my career. Does that mean I did not have any childhood trauma?

Not entirely–there were a couple of things I needed to sort out with my therapist before I eventually had kids. But that aside, my parents being there, albeit aggressively, positively influenced my life. They showed up at school events, cheered me on to do my best, set boundaries and followed through, and molded me to be the *perfect* child. Of course, they could have loosened that leash more, but that's what they knew–and they did the best they could. And thinking back to it, those forced dinners were good for me in the end.

So, when I eventually had kids, I stuck to those dinners. But I tried to make it more fun for them not to view it as a chore. And as a result? I get to know what they are doing and with whom. And the best part is that I don't interrogate them–they willingly offer the information. You might wonder why this quality time with your kids is necessary. Still, as you go through the snippets, I have carefully placed throughout this chapter, you'll understand why being present in your teen's life is crucial.

Becoming Involved in Your Child's Life

"The prevalence of drinking is nearly twice as high among fifteen- to sixteen-year-olds who do not feel close to a parent and among those who do not eat

dinner with a parent, compared with those who do."
–Clinton, White House

Do you think there's a relationship between drug abuse and parental involvement? Well, studies say the link is quite strong. Teens who barely interact with their parents or guardians often resort to doing drugs–that's their way of escaping the emotional turmoil ravaging their souls. That's not to say that being in your teen's life will keep them from ever doing drugs. Instead, it enables you to build a strong relationship with them such that they can open up to you when tempted to do drugs–or when they *actually* do drugs and want a way out. A strong relationship lets your teen know they can count on you, and it all starts with being present. Now, how do you do that without forcing dinners down your kid's throat?

- **Being Respectful:** In chapter six, I emphasized the need to give your teen space. Now, more than ever, they need to have some time for themselves. So, instead of taking this personally, respect it–it's their time to process what they are going through. And most of the time, it has nothing to do with you. But if you keep pushing your teen and barging in, soon enough, it will have something to do with you. So, if you have concerns about their sudden solitude, bring it up respectfully. And if they are not ready to talk about it, let them know you are around when they are.

- **Trust Your Teen:** You've spent more than a decade instilling your values in your child. By now, they know where you stand. You might feel inclined to reiterate your stance just to keep them safe. But you don't have to stand at the door each time they are leaving, ready to give them a talk about sex and drugs. Trust that they know what is right and allow them to make mistakes. Should you ever step in? Sure, when you know that not doing so could harm your child. But that should be for specific events. Your child sleeping in and missing the bus–that's okay, let them learn from it. But empty condom wrappers in their room?–step in.

- **Be Empathetic:** Sometimes, I insist on having dinner with my teenage son, and I can see just how much he wants to get out of it. Maybe he has plans with his girlfriend or wants to watch a game with the boys. I think back to when I had to cancel plans. That meant the world to me because our family dinners were inflexible. So, I give him the night off, which I know makes him happy–I can see it in the way his eyes light up. Then he promises to make it up to me, and that's that. Does that mean I compromise every time? No–our Sunday night dinners are cast in stone. And every child must show up to at least five of the seven dinners in most weeks. It works.

- **Be Understanding:** It's easy to listen to your teen go on about something because you are already armed with an answer. Can you remember the communication blocks we covered in chapter five? Try this: instead of listening to your child, be ready with a solution. Listen to them to understand what they are saying. Ask questions, process what they have said, and think about your answer. Also, not every rant requires an answer or solution–sometimes, your child just wants to talk about something so they can let it go. And if you feel the need to probe because something feels amiss, go the open-ended way. Else, it will feel like an interrogation, and your teen will clam up.

- **Be Present:** When was the last time you spent time with your teen alone? I am not talking about you, the teen, siblings, and other family members. I mean, just you and your teen -that's how you get to see what's going on in their head. Teens are often busy and seem to be pulled left, right, and center. So, they barely have time for you, leaving alone other family members. But if you let them drift away, they can get so far from the shore that you have little of a hold on them. So, how do you reel them in? Well, you do something just for them. Say, for example, your teen enjoys going hiking. Organize one for just the two of you and get to spend one-on-one time with them. These individual sessions, coupled with the family outings, should be enough to build the relationship between you two. Oh, and start slow. If you've not spent much alone time with your teen, start with the easy stuff–going to the movies, picking out something at the mall, etc. And if your teen seems resistant, set some time limits, e.g., they can hang out with you for twenty minutes, then they can go out. That affords them freedom and makes them more open to hangout.

- **Be a Leader:** You are a parent, but that does not make you perfect. But you can try to have more good days than bad. What does that mean? Say, for example, you advocate for no phones at the dinner table. That also includes you! You cannot be on Twitter halfway through the meal, yet your kids have to stay off their phones. What is good for the goose should also be good for the gander. Think of what you've asked your teens to do and lead by example. Want them to be better listeners? – show them. Want them to be on time? – be on time. And when you falter, own up to it, and they will learn that it's okay to be accountable.

- **Embrace Silence:** I was meeting a new friend the other day, and for the first few minutes, we just sat there in silence. She finally muttered, "I don't mind this awkward silence." And I smiled at her, lowering my cup of coffee, feeling understood and even more comfortable. Why?–because spending time with someone does not have to amount to a lengthy conversation. Sometimes, sitting there and being in someone's presence is enough. So, embrace this with your teen. If they want to read a book quietly in the corner as you read a newspaper, embrace it. They are probably just happy being around you without feeling like they need to express it. And if they know they can enjoy quiet time with you, they will feel like they can trust you more–because you're not pushing them to talk when they don't feel like it. Who knows? Your teen could inch closer to you and sit on the next couch.

- **Watch Your Responses:** "You did what?" is probably not the best response to your kid confessing that they drank your wine. Sometimes teens will come to you with minor confessions *just* to gauge your reaction. If you listen to them without passing judgment, they will feel more comfortable telling you about the worse things they have done. For example, your pregnant teen might start by confessing that she had sex. And when you take it in understandingly, seeking to empathize, they can tell you they are pregnant with a child. But suppose you get angry because they had sex, and you ground them. What are the chances that they will talk to you about the baby? Instead, they will probably seek help from someone who will show them where they can get an abortion–which might not be safe. Or they will run away, seek emancipation, or... the list goes on. So, as much as you might feel like responding when your teen confesses, hold back and calm down. Your response affects whether your child ever comes to you again.

- **Remember Their Needs:** A birthday might not seem like a big deal to you. But to your teen, it could feel like the difference between life and death. So, if something is vital to your child, try to make it memorable for them. Say, for example, they have a part in a play and want you there–*be there*. These minor efforts communicate you want to be involved in their life. Then they let you in on more things.

- **Be Supportive:** You might not know this, but teens care about what you think about them. They might shrug off your cheers and act like they are too cool for a congratulatory hug. But studies show that they are still children who want to see their parents cheering them on deep down. So, don't hold back on that "good work." It could be what they wanted to hear all along. Besides, if they have a strong support system at home, they are less likely to be heavily reliant on peer views. One of my friends posted something that stuck with me. She said, *"nothing gives me more confidence than knowing how much love I have waiting for me at home."* It's what keeps her going. So, your words of affirmation could be what your teen needs to fight the societal pressures and reach for their goals.

- **Enforce Discipline:** Does being a supportive parent mean you need to let go of the rod?

  No, you support good behavior and correct that which does not align with positive values. If you hold back on disciplining your child, you communicate that it's okay to keep engaging in destructive behaviors. Sometimes, they even do *just* to see if it will elicit a reaction. So, discipline is the way to go. But you should be careful with it. Start by explaining the need to discipline your child–why are you doing it? Where did they go wrong? What do they have to say about it? It is more effective when you have boundaries in place (check chapter six) so that your teen can know where you draw the line. That way, when they cross it, they will understand why they are losing certain privileges. Remember–we are correcting the behavior and not the person to grow up to be a responsible adult.

- **Don't Mock Your Teen:** You cannot be your child's support system and their taunter at the same time. Say, for example, your child comes to you and says they want to go to Harvard, all giddy about it. Then you scoff at the idea because their grades are not so good. What does that communicate?–that you do not believe in them. So, avoid laughing at your child or taunting them when they make mistakes or come up with ideas. Of course, it's okay to share a laugh with them when they are intentionally funny. But when the joke is at their expense, do not do it.

- **Trust the Process:** Raising a teen takes a lot of work. Even with active listening, leading by example, quality time, and many measures, you could still feel you are fighting a losing war. Guess what? Most parents feel the same way. I've spoken to parents who seem to raise angels, and they, too, do not know what they are doing. So, trust that you have equipped your teen with the right skills. Keep being there, take a deep breath, and give it time.

*"Teens of all ages who eat with their parents, or feel close to their parents, have higher grade point averages. They are more likely to intend to go to college, and they are less likely to have ever been suspended from school." –***Clinton, White House**

Oh yes, being a supportive parent could be the difference between your child excelling in school or their career and flunking. But of course, it's easier said than done–it requires a lot of balance. On one side, you need to be patient, ensuring you are not being pushy. Else, they will isolate you even more. But you cannot be utterly hands-off because you still must step in when they go astray. Knowing when to hold off and take over the reins helps you build that teen-parent relationship.

Are You an Affectionate Parent?

"About fifty percent of fifteen- to sixteen-year-olds who aren't close to their parents have used

marijuana, compared with just twenty-four percent of those close to their parents." –**Clinton, White House**

I mentioned I was brought up in a strict household. And in chapter three, I delved into the different parenting styles and why balancing between a *yes* parent and an authoritarian parent is essential. Growing up in an authoritarian household, I can confirm a critical difference between being present and affectionate. Why? You could be present, yet your child cannot confide in you. I'll give you an example.

When I was around twelve or thirteen, the school heads convened a meeting between the students and the parents. Their main concern? The students were too involved in romantic affairs to pay attention to their schoolwork. After the few grueling hours of listening to our teachers demonize our behavior, I headed home with my parents. We sat at the kitchen table, and I remember my mom saying, "When you finally have a boyfriend, tell us." To an outsider, that must have sounded like a dream come true–parents who were eager to meet the lucky chap. But I knew it was a trap. Never in my wildest dreams would my parents have allowed me to date, and they were just trying to figure out if I was seeing someone. And if I were, they would have probably punished me–I had been punished for way less. So, I nodded, pretending to be oblivious to their scheme, and never dated until I was all but nineteen. Deep down, I wanted to date, but I knew that if I ever *dared* to date, hell would break loose.

Suppose my parents had been affectionate about it. First, they would have sought to understand if I felt somehow about anyone in school. Then they would have walked me through how they felt about dating. And if they had then asked me to introduce them to anyone I liked, I would have known that they were genuinely open to it.

That's just one instance where affection could have made a difference. And you know what? Even when I started seriously dating in my twenties, I was still scared of introducing my partner to my parents. Yes, *terrified*. It's funny when I think about it now–they had instilled the fear of God in me.

So, you can see how easy it is to be heavily involved in your child's life, yet they still cannot open up to you. Are you an affectionate parent? Here are some questions you need to ask yourself:

- **Can your child express a range of emotions around you?** When a parent is affectionate, a teen feels comfortable being themselves. That means they will express their joy and sorrows equally. When they are hurt, they will show it. But when you are not affectionate, your teen feels the need to conceal their true feelings. They dare not show that they are hurt because if you ask them why they are acting differently, they won't know what to say–they do not think you are a safe space to talk about how their boyfriend just dumped them. Or how they feel sad, they failed the tryouts. They fear you will shut them down, distract them, or use any communication blocks we discussed earlier if they express such emotions. So, each time they are around you, they fake their emotions. And if they seem off, they claim to be tired.

- **Does your teen come to you in times of trouble?** Teenage years are full of drama. So, it's somehow expected that your teen will come to you at some point. Maybe they are going through a breakup, having difficulty choosing a school, dealing with a drooping social media following, or even grappling with acne. Whatever it is, your teen should feel comfortable coming to you if they think you will be affectionate. But if they seem to handle everything by themselves, you might not be as affectionate as you think.

- **Can your teen voice their feelings without fear?** Sometimes teens will avoid expressing their true thoughts because they think you will be harsh towards them. For example, your teen might be pro-choice, and you are pro-life. And whenever they try to talk about their views, you shut them down aggressively. Of course, unless your teen is adamant, they will probably take their opinions elsewhere. But shutting down is not the only thing that can hinder your teen from being open. Sometimes, parents overreact to situations. For example, suppose your son comes home and says he was bullied in school, but he has a way to deal with it. And instead of listening to his idea, you march to the bully the next day or the head teacher's office and make a show of it. Do you think your son would open up to you again?

- **Are you careful with your words?** Labeling was quite common when I was growing up. You'd refuse to do something, and suddenly, you were lazy. I've noticed that parents and teachers are more careful with their words nowadays. But that does not mean you might have faltered at some point. Being affectionate requires you to think about the impact of your words. For example, when your teen eats all the cake and you call him greedy, does that make him feel good? No, it makes him feel hurt and judged, not communicating affection. Rather than labeling him, you can explain why it's essential to leave some cake for other people in the home. He will acknowledge his mistake and feel that his behavior was wrong. It's much better than tying him to the behavior.

- **Is your child eager to pursue their talents?** When teens feel supported and loved, they believe they can take up anything that interests them. So, they try almost everything–dancing, sports, drama, etc. Why? Because they know they have a cheerleader at home. But when they feel you will not support them, they hold back. They dare not try the cheerleading team because they know you will not approve of it. And because they are afraid of your reaction, they avoid anything that could trigger it.

- **Can you own up to your mistakes?** That's a big one saying you are sorry and acknowledging that you are not perfect. Somewhere along the way, someone convinced parents they had to be right always. So, even when they were clearly in the wrong, they would not admit it. Of course, this created a rift between the parents and teens. The teens could not understand why they had to observe boundaries and own up to their faults when their parents could not. And do you think this helps the relationship between teens and parents? It does not. Part of being a loving parent boils down to letting go of your ego and embracing that you are human. So, when you lose your cool and yell at your teen, you can admit that you crossed the line and apologize to them.

"Less than thirty percent of teens aged fifteen to sixteen who eat dinner with their parents have been in a serious fight, compared with over forty percent of those who do not eat dinner with their parents." –
Clinton, White House

Have you created a safe space for your teen? Can they trust you with their innermost thoughts and fears? Are there clear boundaries on what's acceptable in the home? These are the building blocks of an affectionate teen-parent relationship. So, as you work on being present, head on to chapter five and start polishing up your communication skills. The goal is not to have mundane dinners where people talk about safe topics. Instead, it is to create such a secure space that your teen can *really* get into what keeps them up at night–be it fears or expectations.

So, open those doors to being a more accepting parent and watch your teen open up to you more. And as we end this chapter, I leave you with one more statistic:

> *"Over fifty percent of teens who do not eat dinner with their parents have had sex by age fifteen to sixteen. By contrast, only thirty-two percent of teens who eat dinner with their parents have ever had sex."*
>
> *–Clinton, White House*

***

About The Author

Taylor DeBruce is passionate about helping people. Her lifetime work as a registered children's nurse, particularly with teenagers, has inspired her to write her debut book. Like other moms, she appreciates how difficult it is to navigate through the teen years and how trying it can be. Also, it is hard to find a solution that fits–parenting is tough. Her book addresses the  many issues that parents will face and offers these solutions. In her spare time, when she's not writing, she can be found working out to her favorite music, traveling, meeting other cultures, as well as preparing gourmet food.